'An admirable and affectionate portrait of a remarkable woman.'
David Welsh, author of *The Rise and Fall of Apartheid*

'"Don't be silly, Nelson!" If you think Margaret Thatcher was the quintessential tough woman politician, try Helen Suzman ... Robin Renwick writes as both friend and historian about this ferociously wonderful woman.'
Libby Purves, *The Times*

'Robin Renwick's biography, which draws on his time as British ambassador in the frenetic last years of white rule, brims with anecdotes. Happily, in an era of overlong and under-edited biographies, it shares her fondness for clarity, concision and humour.'
Financial Times

'The truest of liberals ... this crisp, lucid account is persuasive in presenting her as the doughtiest of fighters for human rights anywhere and one of the finest parliamentarians.'
The Economist

THE END OF APARTHEID

Diary of a Revolution

Robin Renwick

Biteback Publishing

First published in Great Britain in 2015 by
Biteback Publishing Ltd
Westminster Tower
3 Albert Embankment
London SE1 7SP
Copyright © Robin Renwick 2015

ISBN 978-1-84954-792-5

10 9 8 7 6 5 4 3 2 1

A CIP catalogue record for this book is available from the British Library.

Set in Adobe Caslon Pro
Printed and bound in Great Britain by
CPI Group (UK) Ltd, Croydon CR0 4YY

MIX
Paper from
responsible sources
FSC® C020471

CONTENTS

———

INTRODUCTION

———◆———

'If a political leader loses the support of
his followers, it will remain
only for him to write his memoirs'

This book seeks to provide an insider's account of the end of apart-heid, based on a host of meetings which, as British ambassador to South Africa, I had at the time with the main actors in this drama – PW Botha, FW de Klerk, Nelson Mandela, Desmond Tutu – and with many other less well-known figures, who also played important parts in getting rid of a fundamentally abhorrent system sooner and with less bloodshed than most outsiders had dared to hope. There are plenty of heroes in this narrative, along with some cases of pure evil.

Before Nelson Mandela was released from prison, he was told by Helen Suzman of the efforts the British government had been mak-ing to help secure his release. When he was released, he needed and received our help in a number of very practical ways. Above all, he sought our support in helping to overcome problems in the nego-tiations with the government. He did so because he felt that, at this time, we had more influence than others with FW de Klerk and his colleagues, telling me on one occasion that he regarded us as the principal supporters of the negotiating process that, however, was played out entirely between South Africans.

The portrait of Mandela that the reader will find in these pages is not the conventional hagiography. He could be dogmatic and at times distressingly partisan. Egged on by his colleagues in the ANC, he was at times unfair to De Klerk and forgetful of what he owed him. As he confessed to me, he also made a major mistake in failing for nearly a year to meet with Chief Mangosuthu Buthelezi, who had refused to negotiate with the government until Mandela was released.

Yet my admiration for him was second to no one's. Having had the chance to get to know him well before many others, I never ceased to be impressed, and at times amused, at the effect he had on normally hard-boiled visitors, who almost invariably became weak at the knees in the presence of the great man.

As Desmond Tutu observed of him, this diamond had just one flaw, which was to put his trust in colleagues who did not always deserve it. He did so not just out of loyalty, but also from political calculation. Mandela was conscious of the fears of his ANC colleagues in Lusaka that he might start negotiating with the government on his own, and also that the township youth and half his colleagues in the national leadership had more radical agendas than he did. This led him at times to engage in rhetoric and defend positions he did not really believe in, telling me, in one very revealing encounter, that a leader who lost the support of his followers would have nothing better to do than write his memoirs.

Mandela was a far wilier politician, and could be less saintly, than some other portrayals would have us believe, though he did indeed have some saintly characteristics. For at the time there were two Mandelas: in public, much of the time, there was the harshly aggressive, apparently unquestioning spokesman of his party, reading out speeches written by the apparatchiks; and then there was the authentic Mandela, generous in spirit, libertarian by instinct, and inspirational to everyone he met – including me. He used this dual personality quite deliberately to keep his supporters in line behind him. When the chips were down, as in his response to the assassination of Chris Hani, it was the real Mandela who came to the fore.

The reader will find in this account of a series of meetings with him a fundamental difference of approach between Mandela and those of his colleagues whose overriding objective was to win power and hold on to it. Much as he revered the ANC, Mandela, as he showed in government, did not believe in the supremacy of the party over the institutions of the country, including the judiciary and the press. He told Helen Suzman and others that he was relieved that his party did not achieve a two-thirds majority in the first democratic elections, as he wanted there to be no temptation to change the constitution. The least power-hungry of political leaders, he flatly refused to serve more than one term as President.

At the end of every meeting I had with him, he would never fail to ask for money for the ANC, as he was programmed by his colleagues to do. I would explain to him that we provided funding for education, township projects and non-governmental organisations, and not for any political party. Just as he had co-opted his warder in jail and the justice minister, Kobie Coetsee, who kept asking for my help in getting him released, so I found him co-opting me. I was, he kept insisting, his advisor. He also kept urging me to join the ANC. It was, he contended, a broad church 'and you think like us'. This was a debatable proposition.

His next target for co-option was more ambitious. It was in fact the Prime Minister, Margaret Thatcher. He was determined, he told me, 'to get her on my side', and he succeeded in doing so, though not at the expense of her admiration for FW de Klerk.

The reader will also find in these pages a close-up portrait of FW de Klerk as the supposedly conservative leader of the National Party in the Transvaal who, contrary to the expectations of many, including his brother, Willem (Wimpie), set his country on an entirely new path. He did so because, as a clear-sighted, pragmatic and principled person who took his religion seriously, he understood that the status quo could only be maintained by ever-greater violence by the state, and he had developed a visceral dislike of the paramilitary methods of PW Botha and Magnus Malan. There was never any doubt that he believed in civilian control over the military, however hard he found it in practice to exert.

On 2 February 1990, on his way to parliament to deliver his speech unbanning the ANC, the PAC and the South African Communist Party (SACP), he told his wife that South Africa would never be the same. Having made the speech, he told his friends that, as an Afrikaner, he now felt able to look anyone in the eye. The absolute key as to why he launched his country on a new, uncharted course lay in the speech he made in private to the hierarchy of the South African police in January 1990 (see page 110). In it, he said that the

4

alternative to negotiations was for the state to kill thousands more people, which he was not prepared to do, and after this Armageddon, when the shooting stopped, the problem would be exactly the same as it was before it started.

Having unbanned the ANC, released a great number of prisoners and lifted the state of emergency, De Klerk found the country engulfed in a chronic state of unrest as the 'comrades' in the townships flexed their muscles, the ANC continued to fight it out with Inkatha and elements of the security forces contributed to the mayhem.

I never failed to be impressed by De Klerk's resolve in responding to these difficulties. The security forces hated what he was doing. There was a real danger that some of them might actually revolt – as indeed they did in subterranean ways. His own political base was being rapidly eroded.

Yet I never found him contemplating retreat, or what would have been a catastrophic desire to try to stop halfway. Meeting him in his office in parliament or in the Union Buildings, I would find him chain-smoking behind his desk, reacting calmly to the events around him. As I discussed Mandela's concerns with him, including at times when relations between them were badly frayed, I always found him focused on getting to the next stage and never losing sight of the goal, which was to agree a new constitution that would give political rights to all South Africans.

As I pointed out to Mandela on two or three occasions, it is more difficult to negotiate yourself out of power than to negotiate yourself into it. De Klerk did not start off from that position. He would have liked to see more safeguards for minority rights than ended up in the constitution, and he believed and had hoped that a more extended period of power-sharing between the ANC and the National Party would have benefited South Africa. In the midst of this difficult and turbulent process, the influential academic Hermann Giliomee, himself a reformer, but playing devil's advocate, went to see De Klerk to ask why he was making all these changes now. 'You know perfectly well that we could have held out for another ten or twenty years,' said Giliomee, causing De Klerk to get angry. 'Yes, and that would entail killing a lot more people,' he replied, 'and what would we do then?'

De Klerk was criticised for his failure to prevent the security forces from arming Inkatha and contributing in other ways to the violence in the townships. The feeble report of the Harms Commission (see page 154) and the connivance of the army generals allowed even the members of the so-called Civil Cooperation Bureau (CCB) and the unit at Vlakplaas under the infamous Eugene de Kock to continue operating for a while. De Klerk had given repeated orders to terminate all such activities, but they had become endemic in sections of the police and army under his predecessors. It took the appointment of a much tougher judge, Richard Goldstone, and the 'night of the generals' (see page 170) to bring things under better control.

Mandela and his colleagues knew very well that, beneath the superficial deference, important sections of the police and army were flatly opposed to what De Klerk was doing. Joe Slovo and Thabo Mbeki asked me on more than one occasion about the danger of a coup, leading Slovo himself to suggest a period of power-sharing between the ANC and the National Party. Through the transition, De Klerk had to manage the police and army generals as best he could, and in the end succeeded in doing so.

I hope that this book will lay finally to rest the contention that Margaret Thatcher was 'a friend of apartheid' and called Nelson Mandela a 'terrorist' (which, as a matter of fact, she never did). Those who have continued to propagate this myth are going to have to explain away for the next several years, as the archives progressively are opened, the innumerable messages she sent to PW Botha and FW de Klerk urging the release of Nelson Mandela, the repeal of all the apartheid laws and independence for Namibia. She kept up these efforts unrelentingly for ten years after becoming Prime Minister, applying far more pressure, far more directly, on the South African government on these issues than her international counterparts combined, earning from Nelson Mandela the accolade that, despite their differences over sanctions, he and the ANC 'have much to be thankful to her for'. At the time of her funeral, FW de Klerk declared that 'she exerted more influence on what happened in South Africa than any other political leader'.

I am grateful to the Foreign and Commonwealth Office for having permitted me to review all my reports from South Africa, and all the messages exchanged between Margaret Thatcher, PW Botha and FW de Klerk in this period, to help ensure the accuracy of this account.

'Any self-respecting terrorist has an AK-47!'

November 1978

Appointed at this time head of the Rhodesia Department in the Foreign and Commonwealth Office (FCO), I was told that I was being given responsibility for a pretty hopeless cause, but I was to come up with some new ideas.

Ever since Harold Wilson's bizarre assertion in 1966 that economic sanctions would defeat Ian Smith's Unilateral Declaration of Independence (UDI) in 'weeks rather than months', the problem, as Margaret Thatcher put it, had become a 'long-standing cause of grief to successive British governments'.[1] Even US Secretary of State Henry Kissinger had tried and failed to defuse this time bomb.

The Rhodesia crisis had led to a long and bloody guerrilla war, ranging the Rhodesian military against the liberation forces of Robert Mugabe's Zimbabwe African National Union (Zanu) and the military wing of Joshua Nkomo's Zimbabwe African People's Union (Zapu).[2] In 1976, Zanu and Zapu had formed a political-military coalition called the Patriotic Front. The Labour government of James Callaghan, represented by the Foreign Secretary, David Owen, had teamed up with the Carter administration to put forward Anglo-American proposals to resolve the impasse in Rhodesia which were rejected alike by Ian Smith and the Patriotic Front. Ian Smith, meanwhile, was pursuing a so-called internal settlement. Having reached agreement with Bishop Abel Muzorewa and his colleagues, he was planning to hold an election in which the African population would be able to vote for the first time. The Patriotic Front were neither invited nor willing to participate in elections organised by the Rhodesians.

March 1979

Visiting Rhodesia on the eve of the elections, we had to land in Salisbury, the capital, in a sharp twisting spiral, as Nkomo's guerrillas recently had shot down two civilian aircraft of Air Rhodesia with surface-to-air missiles. Within the city, the streets lined with flowering trees gave an impression of calm and orderliness, belied by the fact that travel outside the city after mid-afternoon had become extremely hazardous.

Bishop Muzorewa was likable and well disposed but, manifestly, not really in charge. Even if he had been, he did not appear capable of running a government. I was able to establish a relationship with the person who *was* in charge, General Peter Walls, a charismatic military commander accustomed to leading his men from the front, who had served with the Black Watch and had led a Rhodesian SAS unit during the Malayan Emergency in the 1950s. General Walls was well aware that, while his forces were winning every battle, progressively they were losing the war.

There followed a dinner at Meikles Hotel with the resourceful and cunning head of the Rhodesian Central Intelligence Organisation (CIO), Ken Flower. More lucid than others, he clearly was sceptical that Muzorewa's incorporation in the government would make a difference to the guerrilla war.

I met Robert Mugabe in a broken-down office block in the dilapidated city of Maputo, capital of Mozambique. I did not take, then or later, to his coldly dislikable personality or the extreme aggression of his views. The best course, he declared, was to get on with the war. Negotiations were a waste of time. He was confident that his forces would win in due course. They were doing far more of the fighting than those of Nkomo.

In the Zambian capital of Lusaka, Joshua Nkomo lived in much grander style in a house next to that of his friend and mentor, President Kenneth Kaunda. Nkomo was a mixture of bluster and attempts at charm, with bluster at the time predominating. As he complained bitterly about the failure of the Callaghan government to deliver him to power in Salisbury, I warned that he had better get used to the idea of dealing with the Conservative Party leader, Margaret Thatcher. A few days later, the Rhodesians razed to the ground the villa in which I had met him in Lusaka.

May 1979
On the eve of the general election in Britain, the Conservative Party sent a mission to observe the elections in Rhodesia. It reported positively on the turn-out and clear victory for Muzorewa. At this time, I had never met Margaret Thatcher. But it seemed to me that the

argument that we should not recognise the outcome of the elections in Rhodesia because that would annoy the UN and the Commonwealth had not the faintest chance of being accepted by her. But to recognise a Muzorewa government that attracted no other support and then went under would be a fiasco. Margaret Thatcher just might be prepared to consider a much bolder plan. This would mean Britain playing a far more direct and adventurous role than any previous government had been prepared to contemplate.

Following the Conservative victory, the Foreign Office had greeted with a sigh of relief the appointment of Lord Carrington as Foreign Secretary, after a sometimes turbulent relationship with David Owen. The very patrician Carrington detested the Rhodesian Front and their right-wing supporters in his own party, who regarded Ian Smith (who still bore the scars of the injuries he had suffered while serving as an RAF pilot in Italy during the Second World War) as a kindred spirit and the rebellion he had led against the Crown as a mere peccadillo.

Peter Carrington, who had an even more distinguished war record himself, had no more time for Smith than he did for the bluster of Nkomo and the intransigence of Mugabe, or for the means by which they were seeking to liberate their country. Carrington suspected, as I did, that the former Prime Minister Alec Douglas-Home might well be correct in suggesting that what they wanted was 'one person, one vote – once'.

With a war in progress, the Foreign Office view had been that it would be unwise for Britain to get more directly involved. But, if the situation deteriorated to the point of collapse, we faced the prospect of having to evacuate large numbers of British citizens from Rhodesia in circumstances reminiscent of France's exit from Algeria in 1962. There was, I was convinced, no low-risk policy in relation to Rhodesia.

Margaret Thatcher was surprised to find the Foreign Office advocating a far more muscular approach, which was the opposite of what she had been expecting. The first major decision she was asked to take was that this was going to be a purely British initiative and not an Anglo-American one.

What attracted the Prime Minister most about our plan was its boldness. President Jimmy Carter and his Secretary of State, Cyrus Vance, agreed with undisguised relief that we should take the lead. In the debate on the Queen's speech, the Prime Minister said that 'we intend to proceed with vigour to resolve the issue'. It was a promise not many believed her capable of keeping.

We told her that the constitution of Zimbabwe-Rhodesia (as it was called under the internal settlement) was unlike that on the basis of which we had granted independence to any other former colony, as the real power remained in the hands of the Rhodesian military commanders. She agreed that this must be remedied before the country could be brought to independence.

We then sought to persuade her that bringing the country to independence would not be of much avail, nor would a Muzorewa government survive, if we could not get support from the neighbouring countries and find a way to wind down the war. For this very nasty small war was getting steadily worse. To counter the incursions by Mugabe's guerrillas from Mozambique and Nkomo's from Zambia, the Rhodesians were launching ferocious cross-border raids to disrupt infiltration and destroy the neighbouring countries' infrastructure.

12

They also were arming groups opposed to the Frelimo government in Mozambique, notably the Resistência Nacional Moçambicana (Renamo), fuelling a full-scale civil war in that country. As for Mugabe's tactics, one of the principal methods used to bring areas of the country under his forces' control was the torture, mutilation and execution of village headmen in front of the villagers.

June 1979

At this point the South African foreign minister, Pik Botha, descended on us in London. Pik Botha was one of the most *verligte* (enlightened) members of the South African government, but that was not saying much at the time. He gave Peter Carrington and his deputy, Ian Gilmour, a forty-five-minute lecture on the iniquity of Western policy in southern Africa, alleging constant moving of the goalposts, and allowing precious little time for reply. Bent on revenge, I telephoned 10 Downing Street to ensure that, when Pik Botha saw Margaret Thatcher, he did not get a word in edgeways.

Our next visitor was Bishop Muzorewa. A decent man, he always seemed small and insignificant in meetings, lacking Nkomo's vast girth and bluster and Mugabe's viperish intelligence. Margaret Thatcher told him that there would have to be a new constitution for Zimbabwe-Rhodesia, comparable to those for our former colonies.

July 1979

Our plans for the Commonwealth conference in Lusaka depended on taking the other heads of government by surprise. They were convinced that the Prime Minister planned to recognise Muzorewa.

13

Zambia, including its capital, had been treated as a free-fire zone by the Rhodesian army and air force for many months. As the RAF VC10 neared Lusaka airport, Peter Carrington asked the Prime Minister why she was donning dark glasses. Mrs Thatcher feared that, on arrival, acid might be thrown in her eyes.[3] There was a sharp exchange with Carrington when he suggested that the meeting was going to be a damage limitation exercise, an expression she claimed never to have heard before! It was completely alien to her thinking.

The discussion on Rhodesia, expected to be stormy, was opened by Tanzania's Julius Nyerere. What was needed, he said, was a genuinely democratic constitution and elections in which all parties could participate. The Prime Minister, as we had planned, upstaged him by agreeing. Commonwealth leaders, she said, had never failed to remind us that it was Britain's responsibility to bring Rhodesia to legal independence. That was exactly what we were now intending to do. We would be proposing a new constitution and elections to be held under British control.

The conference ended with the improbable sight of Margaret Thatcher dancing with Kenneth Kaunda. She was far too polite to mention that, on her return to her accommodation one evening, the ceiling had collapsed and there was no running water.

She told the press that the problem was to find a solution that would bring an end to the war. But she added, to my dismay, that she had no plans to send British troops to Rhodesia. This was a decision we were going to have to get reversed.

August 1979

The British government invited Muzorewa and the leaders of the Patriotic Front to a constitutional conference, to be held in London at Lancaster House, that would decide the independence constitution and lay the groundwork for new elections. In the run-up to the conference, Margaret Thatcher agreed that she must not seek to play any part in it, otherwise the participants would constantly be appealing against Carrington to her. This included having nothing whatever to do with Ian Smith, who had been greeted with applause by airport workers on his arrival in Britain and fêted by some right-wing members of her party. Ian Smith could not understand the Prime Minister's refusal to meet him, forgetting that he had led a rebellion against the Queen, which, to Margaret Thatcher, was a capital offence.

A note from Number Ten recorded that Peter Carrington and Thatcher were approaching the conference in 'rather different ways'. The Prime Minister wanted to do everything possible to enable it to succeed. The more worldly-wise Carrington regarded an agreement as 'virtually inconceivable'.[4]

September 1979

Beneath the chandeliers at Lancaster House, Carrington said that the people in the room had it in their power to end the war. After uncompromising statements by Nkomo and Mugabe, the proceedings were interrupted for tea, to force the delegations to mingle with one another. The participants were surprised to see Josiah Tongogara, commander of Mugabe's Zanla forces, greeting Ian Smith and asking about his mother. Tongogara had grown up on Smith's mother's farm:

she had given him sweets as a child. This had not, however, had much effect on his political opinions.

We presented a classic decolonising constitution to both sides, providing for genuine majority rule with protections for minority rights. Muzorewa was overshadowed by the brooding and sardonic presence of Ian Smith, who had driven his country full tilt into an increasingly bloody cul-de-sac. When Smith complained, in his grating voice, that we were dragging out the conference while people were being killed in Rhodesia, the normally imperturbable Carrington lost his temper completely. Purple with anger, he told Smith that the responsibility for the war, which they were losing, rested squarely with him.

Ian Smith's plan was to push the government up against the deadline for the renewal of sanctions in November. Urged by Carrington to find a way to outmanoeuvre him, I told the Rhodesians that not all sanctions depended on the Southern Rhodesia Act, passed in response to UDI, which they knew was unlikely to be renewed in November. A lot of measures existed under other legislation, and these required positive, not merely negative, action to terminate them.

October 1979

This (the threat to continue sanctions) was regarded by Smith as an example of British perfidy. But it had the intended effect. The Muzorewa delegation accepted the proposed constitution, overruling Ian Smith. Nkomo and Mugabe still were holding out, though. To get their attention, we announced that, to organise the elections, we would be sending a British Governor to Rhodesia with full powers, dissolving the Rhodesian government and parliament. As Nkomo and

Mugabe's henchmen said to me, they now realised that, this time, we were serious, which they had never believed we were before.

With extreme reluctance, Muzorewa agreed to stand aside as Prime Minister; a more power-hungry politician would have refused to do so. Nkomo and especially Mugabe, however, still were bent on stringing out the conference while they pushed more of their troops across the border. In the course of many discussions with me at Lancaster House, Mugabe kept telling me that 'power comes from the barrel of a gun' and that he had a PhD in terrorism. The Rhodesians were responding by launching ferocious cross-border raids into Zambia and Mozambique. As Mugabe demanded that we must ensure the release of all political prisoners, I told him that this would have to include his own dissidents, held in a detention camp in Mozambique.

November 1979
Carrington and I were summoned to see the Prime Minister in her room in the House of Commons. We had presented her with a bill providing for Britain to assume direct control of Rhodesia through a Governor with full legislative and executive powers. Reminding us that she was a lawyer, she insisted on going through every line of it.

Next, in the Foreign Office, I spent the mornings with our military representatives negotiating with Ken Flower and Peter Walls and the afternoons with Tongogara and Nkomo's commander, Dumiso Dabengwa, brokering a ceasefire. This required the guerrilla commanders to concentrate their forces in the rural areas in designated assembly places, under the protection of a Commonwealth monitoring force, which, Margaret Thatcher now accepted, would have to be led by the British military. We found an unexpected, invaluable ally in Tongogara, who proved to be far more interested in a peaceful outcome than his political leader, Mugabe. At my suggestion, Christopher Soames, Winston Churchill's son-in-law and Leader of the House of Lords, was persuaded by Carrington to serve as Governor.

Following a series of secret meetings with him in a hotel under the motorway on the Edgware Road, in which he received us clad, bizarrely, in a raincoat, Nkomo told us that he wanted to agree. Mugabe, however, was not going to agree to anything until cornered into doing so.

We warned the Prime Minister that the conference would be dragged out indefinitely unless we took decisive action to bring it to a conclusion. With her approval, we now took the risky step of despatching Christopher Soames to Rhodesia – despite his own misgivings – and lifting sanctions before a ceasefire was agreed.

December 1979

The conference ended with Mugabe still holding out. Through the Mozambican special representative, Fernando Honwana, we were able to persuade President Samora Machel, whose country was suffering desperately from the war, to tell Mugabe that, unless he signed the agreement, there would be no further support from Mozambique. Agreement was announced in time for it to be greeted with applause at the state banquet President Carter was holding for Margaret Thatcher at the White House.

Before our departure from Lancaster House, Tongogara told me that he was taking serious risks in committing to the agreement.

Shortly before the ceasefire was due to be implemented, Mugabe told the British ambassador in Maputo that Tongogara had been killed in a road accident on 26 December as he drove from Maputo to give orders to his forces. His death at this crucial moment gave rise to all sorts of suspicions, the more so as he was known to have had a private meeting with Nkomo before leaving London. His injuries were declared to be consistent with death in a car crash, but, as 'car crashes' have turned out to be a favourite method for the Mugabe regime to maintain itself in power, the jury still is out on what really happened to Tongogara.

On day one of the ceasefire in Rhodesia, those of us who had negotiated the agreement at Lancaster House passed through some of the worst hours of our lives. The monitoring force teams were deployed in remote, guerrilla-infested areas, with the Rhodesians speculating as to how many of them would return. Having put up their flags, they waited for the guerrillas to emerge from the bush. They did so at first in a trickle, which then became a flood, with fifteen thousand men moving into the camps without a single major clash. Mugabe, however, had delivered thousands of lightly armed young *mujiba*s (scouts) to the assembly places, while keeping large sections of his forces outside them. As General Walls protested to me, 'Any self-respecting terrorist has an AK-47!'

January 1980
There followed two months of extreme tension in Rhodesia, with an ever-present risk of a breakdown in the ceasefire, as Mugabe used his forces outside the assembly areas to intimidate the villagers and the Rhodesian special forces contributed their own atrocities, including an

attempt to assassinate Mugabe. Ian Smith engineered a meeting with Muzorewa and the military commanders to demand that they should renege on the agreement and go back to the war. This was rejected by General Walls and Ken Flower. We had got round this corner with screaming tyres.

February 1980

As the elections approached, we received a deluge of international observers, with a great deal of advice and concerns about the turbulent nature of the process. This caused Christopher Soames untactfully to observe: 'This is not Little Puddington in the Marsh. These people think nothing of sticking tent poles up one another's whatnots!'

The CIO chief, Ken Flower, was a legendary figure in Salisbury. Whenever I had dinner with him at Meikles Hotel, the band would play 'Where Have All the Flowers Gone?' I was reassured by him of my own impartiality as he informed me that I was on two death lists, that of some rogue elements of the Selous Scouts, who felt that I was a bad influence on General Walls, and that of Mugabe and his associates, should they lose the election.

We challenged the observer teams to predict the result, which none of them proved able to do. The Rhodesians to the end were over-confident of Muzorewa's support. Nkomo, who knew that his support was confined to Matabeleland, kept urging us to ban Mugabe! Our assessment was that Mugabe would win the largest number of votes, but we did not know how many.

We had asked all the observer missions to declare whether the elections were free and fair *before* the results were declared. Most were reluctant, but the UN representative, Javier Pérez de Cuéllar, showing political courage, declared the election to have been fairly conducted before the outcome was known. He found reassuring, he told us, the sight of shirtsleeved British policemen in their helmets at every polling booth. Even Julius Nyerere acknowledged that 'The British do not know how to rig an election!'

2 March 1980

As the election results came in, but had not yet been announced, and it became clear that Mugabe was going to win, Soames's deputy, Sir Antony Duff, and I set off to Combined Operations Headquarters for what we knew was likely to be a decisive confrontation with the Rhodesian military commanders, with Walls in great distress saying that 'The enemy is about to become our government'. They demanded that we invalidate the elections, with Walls appealing directly to Margaret Thatcher to do so, an approach that was summarily rejected by her. They regretted, they said, ever having gone to Lancaster House.

I reminded them that they had done so only because they were losing the war. Walls, turning to his colleagues, said: 'You know that is true.' He blocked plans by elements of the Rhodesian military to try to stage a coup. Mugabe in turn was persuaded to form a coalition government including Nkomo and Ian Smith's deputy, David Smith, and the British military set about integrating the Patriotic Front and Rhodesian forces. Ken Flower, less surprised at the outcome than his fellow commanders, got himself appointed as Mugabe's head of intelligence. I was presented by Nkomo with an AK-47, which was promptly confiscated by the British military.

May 1980

Margaret Thatcher found it sad that Zimbabwe ended up with a Mugabe government, but political and military realities were on the side of the guerrilla leaders. She shed some tears as she watched on TV the British flag being lowered over Salisbury. I shared her sentiments about Mugabe. But she recognised that the Muzorewa government could not have brought peace to the country and had insufficient support to survive.

She was proud of the role we had played. She had not, initially, wanted to negotiate with Nkomo and Mugabe, but 'unpleasant realities had to be faced'. Britain, she declared, had demonstrated its ability, through 'forceful diplomacy', to settle a particularly intractable international dispute[5] – a success that would not have been possible without her willingness to face all the risks associated with assuming direct control in Rhodesia, which none of her predecessors had been prepared to do.

When, seven years later, I arrived in South Africa as British ambassador, Pik Botha greeted me with the words: 'That was a terrible thing you did at Lancaster House!' Mugabe's victory, he claimed, had set back the cause of reform in South Africa by a generation. I reminded him of his own statement to us at the time that Rhodesia was on its beam ends. The longer negotiations were delayed, the more radical the outcome was likely to be – a principle that did not apply only to Rhodesia.

CHAPTER I

❦

'This time we have locked up all the right people!'

July 1987

Despatched by Margaret Thatcher to be the British ambassador to South Africa, I found the country in the grip of severe repression under the regime of President PW Botha. Nelson Mandela and his senior colleagues were in prison with no prospect of release. The other leaders of the African National Congress (ANC) were in exile. The ANC and Pan Africanist Congress (PAC) were banned. Two and a half thousand people had been detained without trial. The press were censored and a state of emergency was in force.

It had to be said that, in the short term, these tactics were working, in the sense that the crackdown was effective and 'order' had been restored. When I asked General Johann van der Merwe, head of the security police, why, at this point, the country was quiet, he replied cheerfully: 'This time we have locked up all the right people!'

Intensely frustrated by the obstructionist attitude of PW Botha, in sending me to South Africa Margaret Thatcher wanted to see us playing a more activist role than the embassy hitherto had done, having been encouraged by the Foreign Office to engage in her least favourite activity – damage limitation. As we had a large number of British citizens in South Africa, by far the largest investments and close links with the English-speaking business community, she found it frustrating that Britain apparently had so little influence on the regime.

She had been subject to attack, in a series of Commonwealth conferences, for her resistance to more extensive sanctions against South Africa. We had, in fact, imposed military, nuclear, oil and sports sanctions, but she was adamantly opposed to blanket sanctions which, in her opinion, would further reinforce the siege mentality of the Afrikaners as well as destroy the livelihoods of large numbers of black South Africans. She regarded many of the leaders calling on her to take these steps as a bunch of hypocrites, given, as she put it, their own imperfect records on human rights and dependence on trade with South Africa.

As for her own views on apartheid, she had alarmed the South Africans by writing in 1983 to the Conservative MP Ian Lloyd that the exclusion of blacks from the political process was 'a powerful factor in compelling black politicians to seek by violence what is denied to them by the laws under which they live'.[6]

June 1984

Three years earlier, President Botha had travelled to Europe for the fortieth anniversary of the 1944 Normandy landings – ironically, as he had opposed South Africa's participation on the side of the Allies in the Second World War. Being a believer in engagement rather than ostracism, Margaret Thatcher invited him to meet her at Chequers, the Prime Minister's official country residence. The veteran anti-apartheid campaigner, Archbishop Trevor Huddleston, met her to urge her not to see Botha. She replied that she wanted to tell Botha face to face that South Africa must change, which is what she proceeded to do.

In her briefing notes, heavily underlined by her, she was forewarned that PW Botha was hard, dour, belligerent and intolerant of criticism. In their private meeting, he complained that he never received any credit for the improvements he had made in the conditions of black South Africans. In return he got a forthright lecture about the continuance of forced removals of black South Africans from areas reserved for the whites. She pressed him on the continued detention of Nelson Mandela, subsequently confirming in parliament that she had done so.

PW Botha demanded that the ANC office in London should be closed. Mrs Thatcher said that we could not do this under our law. There was no evidence that the office personnel were guilty of illegal activities.[7] In fact, the UK authorities were more worried about the actions of South African embassy personnel, two of whom had just been expelled for organising break-ins at the offices of the ANC and the South West Africa People's Organisation (Swapo). In March 1982, there had been a bomb explosion at the ANC office, which subsequently turned out to have been the work of Craig Williamson, a senior figure in the security police.

Pik Botha's summary of what the South Africans took away from the meeting was that, 'while her manner remained sympathetic, Mrs Thatcher went on to say very firmly that the key issues were still pressing: apartheid had to be dismantled, Mandela and other prisoners released and the front-line states should be spared further attacks by the South African armed forces. The forcible removal of urban blacks had to stop.' But they did get the impression, correctly, that Mrs Thatcher was sympathetic to the linkage between South African withdrawal from Namibia and the withdrawal of Cuban forces from Angola.[8]

Her Foreign Secretary, Geoffrey Howe, observed that the Bothas probably were surprised to be pressed by her on all the key issues: 'Apartheid must go. Mandela (and others) be set free and the front-line states no longer exposed to attack from South Africa.' Forced removals also must come to an end.[9]

Having heard Margaret Thatcher's remarks on television immediately after the meeting, Trevor Huddleston sent her a handwritten note, thanking her in fulsome terms and saying that her public statement had given him encouragement and hope: 'It was truly all I could have wished for.' She replied that she had expressed her concern at the continued detention of Nelson Mandela and the need for early progress on this.[10]

Margaret Thatcher had, for a while, entertained the hope that PW Botha was serious about reform, for he had stated in 1979 that South Africa must 'adapt or die'. The pass laws, intended to keep the black population from establishing permanent residence in the urban areas, at last were abolished, as they had proved simply unenforceable. The prohibition of mixed marriages was lifted as well. But Botha's objective was to modernise apartheid, not to get rid if it. His much-heralded constitutional reform involved the creation of new separate chambers in parliament for the Indian and coloured communities. The exclusion of the black community from the so-called tricameral parliament triggered a wave of unrest within the townships which had led to the imposition of a state of emergency. Opposition to the proposed constitutional reforms led to the formation of the United Democratic Front (UDF) to organise black resistance within the country.

August 1985

PW Botha was due to make a speech in Durban on 15 August that was advertised in advance by Pik Botha as representing the 'crossing of the Rubicon'. Rejecting the reformist language in the text presented to him, PW Botha delivered instead a characteristically finger-wagging performance. 'Don't push us too far,' he declared. He was not, he said, prepared to lead white South Africans 'on a road to abdication and suicide'.

Immediately following the 'Rubicon' speech, a consortium of US banks, led by Chase Manhattan, announced the decision, already taken in principle, to refuse to roll over the country's debts or to make any further loans to the government. A host of other international banks followed suit. FW de Klerk observed subsequently that the Governor of the South African Reserve Bank, Gerhard de Kock, regarded the speech as having cost South Africa one million rand for every word.[11] This was a massive underestimate. For these market sanctions were to prove far more effective than any other measures against South Africa, apart from the arms embargo.

October 1985

The Commonwealth heads of government, meeting in the Bahamas, had decided to send a group of 'eminent persons', led by General Olusegun Obasanjo of Nigeria and the former Prime Minister of

Australia, Malcolm Fraser, to South Africa to explore ways of trying to get negotiations under way with representatives of the black majority. On 31 October, Margaret Thatcher wrote to PW Botha urging him to accept the Commonwealth mission and stating that the release of Mandela would have more effect than any other action he could take. The seven-member Eminent Persons Group received some encouragement from Pik Botha and met Mandela in prison. But PW Botha had been persuaded to allow them to visit only under pressure from Thatcher. Adamantly opposed to outside interference, he decided to 'get rid of these people'. On 19 May 1986, he did so by ordering the South African Defence Force (SADF) to launch air attacks on Gaborone, Harare and Lusaka, ostensibly against ANC targets, bringing an abrupt end to the Commonwealth's negotiating efforts.

July 1986

Margaret Thatcher had tried to persuade Geoffrey Howe to join the Commonwealth mission, untactfully suggesting that she could do his job as well as hers while he was away. He had resisted successfully but, extremely reluctantly, he was pushed by the Prime Minister to try again, this time on behalf of the European Community (EC). His reluctance, as she acknowledged, proved justified, as he was berated on television by Kenneth Kaunda and received boorishly by PW Botha, who was beside himself, denouncing 'damned interfering foreigners'.[12]

CHAPTER II

---◆---

'The greatest risk is not taking any risks'

It was made clear to the South African government that I was being sent there as the Prime Minister's appointment. That, I hoped, would give me some leverage with the regime. For they could hardly afford the complete withdrawal of her support, though they had been doing precious little to deserve it.

Margaret Thatcher, at the time, was riding high, having just won a third consecutive election victory in Britain. Having formed a special relationship with the Soviet leader, Mikhail Gorbachev – whom she famously had declared in 1984 a man she could do business with – she had made, before the election, a triumphal visit to Moscow, where the British press could not believe the size of the crowds that had turned out to greet her. She had used her visit to tell Gorbachev that she was looking to him to change Soviet foreign as well as domestic policy. She found it all the more exasperating that the South African government was so impervious to her influence.

July 1987

On the day before leaving for South Africa to take up my post, I was summoned to meet the Prime Minister. She had been urged by, of all people, Robert Mugabe to visit South Africa. There was no point, she agreed, in doing so unless conditions fundamentally changed, including the release of Mandela. Only if she could get the kind of results achieved in Moscow with Gorbachev would she be prepared to go to South Africa.

Margaret Thatcher agreed that, while we should continue to defend our economic interests, we should never put ourselves in the position of appearing to expect, still less to rely on, the present South African government to do the right thing. They were far more likely to do the wrong thing.

On Senator Robert Dole's advocacy of support for the Renamo rebel movement in Mozambique, the Prime Minister said that she would tell the Americans that the right policy was to support President Joaquim Chissano, who had replaced Samora Machel following the latter's death in a plane crash. Samora Machel had been effusive in thanking Thatcher for her success in resolving the Rhodesia dispute and had won her support for Mozambique to join the Commonwealth. She commented that the South Africans had been playing a double game over Renamo.

She agreed with my main suggestion, which was that I should tell PW Botha on her behalf in the clearest terms that any major cross-border raids in the run-up to the next Commonwealth conference would make her position intolerable and result in the withdrawal of her support. She concluded grimly that there was no early prospect of political progress.

30

In her sole meeting with him, she had found PW Botha charmless and inflexible, but she remained convinced of the importance of dialogue with other members of his government. As in her dealings with the Soviet Union, she was looking for a successor who might be prepared to set out on a different course. If I found anyone who fitted that description, I was to give him all possible encouragement.

* * *

Arriving in Cape Town, I was greeted by Pik Botha, the irrepressible South African foreign minister, with recriminations about Lancaster House. I said that, without an agreement, there would have been a military collapse in Rhodesia, and that had been the South African assessment as well.

Pik Botha, changing tack, cheerfully agreed. He thought Mugabe would have preferred to come to power by military means and probably would have succeeded in doing so. The South African government had told the Rhodesians that they were not prepared to take over the war. Smith should have negotiated earlier. But Britain must understand the fundamental differences between South Africa and Rhodesia.

I said that we did understand them. Wherever the South Africans ended up, it was not going to be at Lancaster House. Britain had no constitutional responsibility for South Africa. A settlement could only be achieved between South Africans.

On the Commonwealth conference, I said that the Prime Minister was never worried about being alone when convinced that our position was right, but any more actions like the ones that had scuppered the Eminent Persons mission would produce a reaction from her. Pik Botha said that he had been trying to improve relations with Mozambique. I warned against continuing South African support for Renamo, which of course he denied was taking place.

August 1987

Before presenting my credentials to PW Botha, I arranged to have a drink with Ton Vosloo, head of the leading Afrikaans press group, the Nasionale Pers (now Naspers). I did so because, before arriving in South Africa, I had resolved to concentrate my efforts on the Afrikaners and the black leadership, rather than falling into the easy trap of consorting mainly with the more liberal elements of the English-speaking community, who, despite their best efforts, clearly were not able to have a decisive influence on events.

I told Vosloo that Margaret Thatcher did understand the concerns of white South Africans and the historic dilemma confronting the Afrikaners. But, as friends of South Africa, we were concerned that PW Botha was driving his country into a cul-de-sac and at the increasing militarisation of the regime. In making public statements about the kind of changes we would like to see come about, I hoped that these might be carried in the Afrikaans press, especially *Beeld* and *Die Burger*, and not only in the English-speaking papers. Vosloo promised that the Afrikaans press would carry the Prime Minister's views. He advised me to make some gesture to the Afrikaners. This I attempted to do, despite my own imperfect knowledge of the language, by delivering part of my credentials speech in Afrikaans. It duly was carried on the state-controlled television.

In this, my first encounter with PW Botha, he expressed appreciation for the phrases in Afrikaans, which he took as showing that we
had some understanding of the Afrikaner predicament. I said that
the Prime Minister did understand this, but was no less concerned
about political rights for the black population. At the Commonwealth
conference in Vancouver, scheduled for October, she would be facing
pressures for general sanctions. If there were further raids of the kind
that had put an end to the Commonwealth mission, he should not
count on her support. There should be no misunderstanding between
us about this.

PW Botha said that he registered the point, but some neighbouring states were helping the ANC to launch terrorist actions into South
Africa. He then complained about the ANC office in London. I said
that, as the Prime Minister had told him when she had met him at
Chequers, the office was permitted to operate in London, provided it
did so within the law.

As in all my meetings with PW Botha, who never forgot that his
mother had been interned by the British during the Anglo-Boer War,
this one was conducted with the two of us alone in a small study in
the Tuynhuys. His domed bald head and tinted glasses gave him an
eerie appearance, accentuated by the fact that our meetings took place
in semi-darkness, lit only by a small green lamp on his desk, conjuring
up images of what it must have been like calling on the *Führer* in his
bunker.

The 'Groot Krokodil' (Big Crocodile), as he was less than affec-
tionately known by supporters and enemies alike, was prone to furious
outbursts of temper that left many of his ministers frankly terrified

of him. On 6 September 1966, the day his leader, Hendrik Verwoerd, had been assassinated, he had confronted Helen Suzman in parliament, 'arms flailing and eyes bulging', yelling at her that 'you liberalists are responsible for this'. In a prior meeting with him, opposition leader Frederik van Zyl Slabbert had remarked that Chief Buthelezi wanted to be the 'only bull in the kraal', only for PW Botha to release the supposedly private tape recording of their meeting. Before each of my encounters with Botha, I made a silent vow that it was not going to be in his interests to release the transcripts of any of his conversations with me.

The deputy foreign minister, Kobus Meiring, invited me to meet a dozen young National Party MPs who, he assured me, were reform-minded. The result was a very interesting and encouraging encounter with Roelf Meyer, Sam de Beer, Leon Wessels, Renier Schoeman, David Graaff and others, most of whom were to serve in the government of FW de Klerk.

A meeting with Chris Heunis, the Minister for Constitutional Development – or rather the lack of it – had the opposite effect. His hopes of succeeding PW Botha had been destroyed by Denis Worrall, who had resigned from his post as the South African ambassador in London to run for parliament as an independent, challenging Heunis and very nearly defeating him in his Helderberg constituency in the 1987 elections. With a lugubrious walrus moustache, unmatchable pomposity and a visceral dislike of the British, Heunis warned that no interference by Mrs Thatcher in South Africa's affairs would be tolerated.

As I drove each morning to the embassy in Cape Town along the magnificent Rhodes Drive, which bisects the campus of the University of Cape Town, I would encounter from time to time groups of students skirmishing with the riot police. The sympathies of the outraged motorists were by no means with the students. The courageous vice chancellor of the university, Dr Stuart Saunders, frequently was to be found standing in the middle of these disturbances.

The embassy itself, reflecting our shared history, was to be found in the government complex, immediately opposite parliament and the President's office. This caused great annoyance to PW Botha, who sent me an envoy requesting us to move. In reply I inquired whether the South Africans had any intention of moving South Africa House from Trafalgar Square.

I made a pilgrimage to Stellenbosch to meet the undisputed leader of the Afrikaner business community and great philanthropist, Anton Rupert. The extraordinary business acumen of this self-made billionaire was equalled by his no less extraordinary modesty. We would have lunch with a minimum of fuss in the local restaurant, where he appeared to be positively revered. When I asked him if he could not use his influence with PW Botha to propel him in a more positive direction, he showed me an exchange of messages with the President in which he had made the same argument in the politest possible terms, only for Botha to take no notice whatsoever.

His English-speaking counterpart, Harry Oppenheimer, had served as an opposition member in the South African parliament, had supported Helen Suzman when she sat as the sole MP opposed to apartheid and had sought to set an example to other South African companies in terms of the reformist political stance of the Anglo American Corporation. That said, as he told me himself, he did not

believe that he or Anglo American or the business community had
any influence on PW Botha at all.

I sought to befriend two South Africans I greatly admired and who
were to remain close friends of mine to the end of their lives: Helen
Suzman and Van Zyl Slabbert. Helen Suzman and I were returning
from our first lunch together when, as we entered the parliamentary
precinct, an Afrikaner guard peered into the car. Recognising Helen
and then me, he backed away. 'Can't you see the balloon coming out of
his head? Conspiring with the enemy,' Helen laughed.

The politics of the white community remained quite tribal. There
was no direct relationship between Helen Suzman and the *verligte*
Afrikaners, but some of them were starting to make speeches about
the unworkability of various aspects of apartheid that sounded eerily
like the speeches she had made many years before. In 1986, at the time
of the repeal of the pass laws, a National Party MP, Albert Nothnagel,
declared that she had been proved to have been right all along.

Frederik van Zyl Slabbert had been the charismatic leader of the
Progressive Federal Party, and had infuriated Suzman by abruptly
deciding to resign from parliament to pursue extra-parliamentary
efforts to engage in serious discussions with the ANC. Together with
Alex Boraine, Van Zyl Slabbert formed a think-tank, the Institute for
a Democratic Alternative for South Africa (Idasa), and his efforts cul-
minated in the historic meeting between a group of mainly Afrikaner
intellectuals and Thabo Mbeki and his colleagues in Dakar in June
1987. Van Zyl Slabbert was denounced for his pains by PW Botha
as one of Lenin's 'useful idiots'. Helen Suzman had been angered by
his decision to stand down from parliament, thereby damaging his

party. Helping to achieve a reconciliation between the two of them was scarcely less challenging than persuading the government to start talking to the ANC.

In Johannesburg and Pretoria I met three other Afrikaners who were to become both friends and powerful allies. The first of these was Pieter de Lange, head of the Broederbond, the secret society that linked together the Afrikaner elite. For decades, this had been regarded by outsiders as exerting a sinister influence. It was true that the Broederbond was dedicated to the promotion of Afrikaner interests – above all, culture – and was one of the mainstays of the regime. Pieter de Lange, however, had circulated to the members of the society a remarkable discussion document in which he invited them to think the unthinkable. Suppose, it said, there was an African majority in parliament and in government one day: how then could Afrikaner interests be protected? Warning clearly of the impossibility of preserving the status quo, the document contained the striking phrase, 'the greatest risk is not taking any risks'.

De Lange described a long discussion he had had with Thabo Mbeki at a conference in New York in 1986. ANC president Oliver Tambo also had been asking to see him. De Lange was scathing about Dr Andries Treurnicht and the Conservative Party (CP), whose members had been trying to paralyse any thinking about the future in the Broederbond. His view was that the Group Areas Act and the Separate Amenities Act would have to go. PW Botha thought exclusively in terms of Afrikaner interests; he would not allow Mandela to die in jail, but would go on insisting on an absolute renunciation of violence. De Lange's conviction was that there would have to be a historic compromise between Afrikaner and black nationalism and that this would have to come sooner rather than later.

I said that it seemed to me that the one encouraging feature of the situation was the intensity of the debate within Afrikanerdom about the direction reform should take. Although not numerically strong, people like Hermann Giliomee, Willie Esterhuyse and FW de Klerk's brother, Wimpie, represented an important fraction of the intellectual elite in a society which paid more homage to professors than we did in Britain!

There followed a meeting with the head of the Dutch Reformed Church, Professor Johan Heyns. I was to spend many hours with him at his modest bungalow in a suburb of Pretoria. Professor Heyns had declared apartheid a heresy, thereby splitting his church and provoking the fury of the conservatives. He was to prove the most effective of allies in a series of tight corners over the next four years. He was assassinated in November 1994 by a right-wing gunman while playing cards with his granddaughter in the house where he had received me with such kindness.

The Bank of England had impressed upon me the high regard in which they held the Governor of the South African Reserve Bank, Gerhard de Kock. I found him pessimistic about South Africa's economic prospects. He was predicting 2 per cent growth in the economy for 1987 and 1988 – not enough to keep pace with the increase in population. This weakness he saw as the result of PW Botha's stop/go attitude to political reform. He was determined that South Africa must honour its debts. But the refusal of the Western banks to extend any further credit meant that the country was obliged to export capital to pay down its debts, rather than importing capital to fund its development.

When I arrived in South Africa, relations with the leaders of the UDF were strained because of the British government's opposition to sanctions. It was obvious that greater efforts needed to be made by us to get much closer to the future leadership of the country. Some of the younger members of the embassy and consulates had good contacts in the townships. I encouraged them to give an over-riding priority to developing these. It was difficult and sometimes hazardous but very rewarding work, which they did to such effect that they became known as the 'township attachés'.

It was not possible to send young members of the embassy into the townships, still less to visit them myself, as I aimed most weeks to do, without doing more to help the people living there. First Chris Patten and then Lynda Chalker, as the ministers in charge of overseas aid, allocated the relatively modest sums needed to enable us to support, eventually, over three hundred projects in Soweto, Mamelodi, Crossroads, Gugulethu and many of the other townships and squatter camps in the Cape and the Transvaal. These projects, amazingly, were controversial at the time, as it was argued by various anti-apartheid campaigners outside South Africa that this was merely ameliorating apartheid and, therefore, postponing the day of reckoning. This doctrine of 'worse is better' did not appeal to me. Above all, it did not appeal to people in the townships, who desperately needed help and support. Virtually all the projects we supported were run by determined opponents of the regime, and when their parties were unbanned we discovered what we knew already – that we had established contact with most of the internal leadership of the ANC and PAC.

I tried also to establish friendships with a number of ex-Robben Islanders who had served long sentences in prison with Mandela, including Neville Alexander, who made the film *Robben Island Our University*. Several of those who had been released belonged to the Africanist tradition, including Fikile Bam and Dikgang Moseneke, both of whom went on to distinguished legal careers in the post-apartheid era – Moseneke as Deputy Chief Justice. In Soweto, Dr Nthato Motlana continued to play a prominent role on behalf of the ANC, and I made regular visits to Albertina Sisulu. I also tried to show all the support I could for the Delmas treason trialists, Popo Molefe and Mosiuoa 'Terror' Lekota, by attending sessions of their trial, and was rewarded with their friendship when they eventually were released.

In Johannesburg, I made contact with Cyril Ramaphosa, leader of the National Union of Mineworkers (NUM), at the time in the thick of a miners' strike. Ramaphosa, a redoubtable negotiator, assured me that he had no intention of 'doing a Scargill' and destroying his own union (Arthur Scargill had led the British mineworkers to defeat in a year-long confrontation with the government of Margaret Thatcher in 1984–85). After he had extracted all the concessions he could, one week later the strike was settled.

As our purpose was to persuade the government to talk to the real black opposition leaders, we sought to use the embassy and consulates as a proving ground for this. A number of Robben Islanders became regular visitors to the embassy, as did a number of National

Party MPs. We invited representatives of both groups to the embassy, without telling them who else might be there. This led at first to one or two difficult moments, but not for long, as they became accustomed to these encounters and found that there was plenty to discuss. For those who had been imprisoned at one time or another did want to tell those in or close to authority about their experiences, the effects on them and their families of the apartheid laws, including the still-segregated schools and residential areas, and their political demands. There were by now people in positions of real power and influence in Afrikaner society and on the fringes of government, or among its younger elements, who wanted to know whom in fact they were going to be dealing with. Some at least among them could hardly fail to be impressed by the qualities of those the regime had condemned to years of imprisonment for their political acts and views.

There followed a meeting with PW Botha's chief henchman, the Minister of Defence, Magnus Malan, leader of the group of so-called securocrats – key ministers and senior defence, police and intel-ligence chiefs – surrounding the President. A former Chief of the SADF, Malan was the leading proponent of the theory of the 'total onslaught' against South Africa by the Soviet Union and its allies. Though careful not to give written orders to this effect, Malan was a great believer in 'taking out' enemies of the regime, internally through special force units, which had developed into assassination squads, and externally by whatever means were necessary. He had received from PW Botha our warning about cross-border raids, but contended that he had to defend South Africa against terrorist groups poised to cross the borders. I said that of course he would defend the borders, but

the air strikes on neighbouring capitals that had put an end to the
Commonwealth Eminent Persons Group's visit had not hit any ANC
targets at all.

Malan claimed that, in Mozambique, Renamo were not getting
help from the South African military. I said that, if that were so,
they most certainly were getting help from others in South Africa.
He expressed concern about the major Angolan offensive, involving
the Cubans and Russians, being mounted against Unita leader Jonas
Savimbi's base at Jamba, in the southeast of the country. The Angolans
had a vast amount of heavy equipment and air defence missiles supplied by the Russians, posing military problems for South Africa. I
had little doubt that the very capable South African forces operating
inside Angola, with their own air support, would stop the Angolan
advance. But, clearly, the war there was becoming more costly for the
South Africans.

September 1987

I had a first meeting with FW de Klerk, leader of the National Party
in the Transvaal, and then Minister of National Education. De Klerk
was reputed to be a very conservative figure, but I found him to be
open, friendly and impressively self-confident. He knew, he said, of
my involvement in the Rhodesia settlement. He wanted me to know
that, if he had his way, South Africa would not make the same mistake
the Rhodesians had. What was the mistake, I asked. 'Leaving it far too
late to negotiate with the real black leaders,' was the reply.

The Separate Amenities Act, he said, would be repealed in due
course. The Group Areas Act could not be repealed immediately,

because of the concerns of poorer whites, who were disposed to vote for Treurnicht and his colleagues in the Conservative Party. As sports minister (1978–79) he had abolished apartheid in sport, only for the international sports sanctions to remain in place.

I made the journey to the Zulu capital, Ulundi, to meet Chief Mangosuthu Buthelezi, Chief Minister of Kwazulu. He had rejected the government's offer of 'independence' for his homeland and insisted that he would not negotiate until Mandela was released. The ANC and Buthelezi's party, Inkatha, were engaged in a bloody struggle for power and territory in Natal, with Inkatha predominant in the quasi-feudal rural areas and the ANC among Zulu youths in the townships.

Visiting Buthelezi in his stronghold at Ulundi was like stepping back in time. On ceremonial occasions he was to be found brandishing a battle axe and wearing a necklace of lions' teeth, but these accoutrements disguised a very sharp mind indeed. He was intensely conscious and proud of the history of the Zulu nation, reminding me that he had himself played the role of King Cetshwayo in the 1964 film *Zulu*, which also starred a young Michael Caine.

He knew the Prime Minister well, having been introduced to her by the writer Sir Laurens van der Post. She found Buthelezi's views on sanctions and the armed struggle far more compatible than those of the ANC. Laurens van der Post, who was a friend of the Prime Minister and of the Prince of Wales, believed that the Zulus were the key to the future of South Africa. In an attempt to broaden his horizons, I arranged for him also to meet Thabo Mbeki, but Laurens dismissed the pipe-smoking Thabo as unacceptably westernised. When she asked me about Laurens's opinions, I told Margaret

43

Thatcher that, while Buthelezi had strong support in Natal and among the Zulu mineworkers on the Witwatersrand, Mandela and the ANC had nationwide support. There could be no settlement without them, as Buthelezi himself recognised.

In this meeting, Buthelezi said that the problem was defeating two evils – poverty and apartheid, not just apartheid. The experience of neighbouring Mozambique showed the futility of liberation coupled with economic ruin. Apartheid was doomed, but ANC bombs pushed white South Africans deeper into the laager. They were attacking the state at its strongest point. After twenty-five years of ANC attacks, there were no 'liberated zones'; not even a single bridge had been destroyed. He would continue to seek genuine negotiations through an inclusive *indaba* (discussion). He had just rejected the latest attempts by the government to draw him into negotiations on their proposed National Council. They wanted black representation, but only in a purely advisory role.

CHAPTER III

'Let us pray'

October 1987

I had my first meeting with Archbishop Desmond Tutu, of whom I was a wholehearted admirer. He had been boycotting my predecessor because of his disagreement with the British government about sanctions. So, before setting off for South Africa, I went to Lambeth Palace to see the Archbishop of Canterbury, Dr Robert Runcie, who knew of my involvement in the Rhodesia negotiations. I asked him on that basis to point out to Desmond Tutu that I could hardly be regarded as a supporter of apartheid, which he kindly agreed to do.

Each meeting with Desmond Tutu would open with the words, 'Let us pray', with both of us falling to our knees. After I got to know him better, I suggested that this was his way of letting me know that there were three of us in the room and I was outnumbered. In reality, he was absolutely right. For with South Africa at the time in the grip of PW Botha and General Malan, who had created the CCB, a secret

45

paramilitary unit to eliminate enemies of the regime, there was indeed plenty to pray about.

Desmond Tutu said that he knew I was not a believer in general sanctions. He was an advocate of sanctions only because he could see no alternative. 'Constructive engagement', the phrase coined by US envoy Dr Chester Crocker, had failed. Tutu felt that Britain's opposition to sanctions was based on our commercial interests. I said that our economic interests and jobs in Britain were indeed a factor in our attitude to sanctions. But there were other factors too. If we had agreed that Europe should ban the import of fruit and vegetables from South Africa, this would have been liable to put a hundred thousand non-whites out of work, rendering with their dependants half a million people destitute. If we believed that further sanctions would cause apartheid to be removed within two or three years, I had no doubt that we would impose them. But we did not believe that. People who lost their jobs would be out of work for the foreseeable future, as Tutu himself acknowledged.

I added that, if comprehensive sanctions were imposed, the economy of Zimbabwe would collapse long before that of South Africa, as would the economies of Botswana, Lesotho and Swaziland. If companies like BP and Shell left, their health, welfare, education, training, pensions and scholarships programmes would be lost. I did not expect him to agree, but I did ask him to accept that our opposition to general sanctions was sincerely based.

I gave him details of our assistance to Mozambique. He said that President Chissano had spoken to him about this. He knew that the Prime Minister had advised the Americans against support for

Renamo. I explained that we also had launched a US$20 million programme to provide scholarships for black South Africans. We also were giving direct help to a lot of church and community group projects in the townships. I needed help from him on this, as some of the external anti-apartheid organisations were contending that this was simply 'ameliorating apartheid'. Tutu promised his support for the projects. He continued to decline to meet US and British representatives so long as their governments opposed additional sanctions, but decided to waive this ban so far as I was concerned.

I was able to start establishing a particularly close relationship with the South African Director-General for Foreign Affairs, Neil van Heerden, one of the most outstanding public servants I ever encountered, in his own or any other country. He assured me of his determination, and that of Pik Botha, to make progress at long last towards a solution of the Namibia dispute. Pik Botha, he said, genuinely wanted to work towards a normalisation of relations with Mozambique, an eventual signature by South Africa of the Nuclear Non-Proliferation Treaty and the release of Mandela.

I had a further discussion with Buthelezi focused on a message he had sent to PW Botha pointing out the consequences of Mandela's dying in prison, and saying that his release was the key to unblocking the political situation. It would be impossible to get a real negotiation going while Mandela remained in jail.

The fighting between Inkatha and the ANC had led to over four hundred deaths around Pietermaritzburg in Natal. The Prime Minister had told Buthelezi that she wanted efforts made to bring the violence to an end. We supported efforts by his deputy, Oscar Dhlomo, to reach an agreement with the UDF about this. In Lusaka, Thabo Mbeki knew that Mandela was in favour of mending fences with Buthelezi. Buthelezi said that he accepted Mbeki's bona fides and those of Oliver Tambo. But Chris Hani, head of Umkhonto we Sizwe (MK), the military wing of the ANC, had said publicly that it was the policy of MK to seek to assassinate members of the Inkatha Central Committee, including Buthelezi. He regarded the ANC's attempts to overthrow the government by force as futile. But the ANC was not going to melt away and nor was Inkatha.

The finance minister, Barend du Plessis, had reached the same conclusions about South Africa's financial situation as Gerhard de Kock. The capital outflow had somehow to be reversed. Du Plessis had the reputation of being more *verlig* than De Klerk, as did several of his colleagues. But the South African government still was under the iron hand of PW Botha, who exercised a reign of terror over the cabinet. He believed in intimidation across the board. At this time, infuriated one evening by the television news, he telephoned the South African Broadcasting Corporation (SABC) to get the news changed in the middle of the programme!

Margaret Thatcher, meanwhile, had been attending the Commonwealth conference in Vancouver, at which she felt that the Canadian hosts were trying to play to the African gallery. She flatly opposed any sanctions that would cause mass unemployment, telling Robert Mugabe that 80 per cent of Zimbabwe's trade passed through South Africa and that one million Zimbabweans lived and worked there. At the end of the conference, she was asked by a journalist about a statement by the local representative of the ANC that, if she continued to oppose sanctions, British businesses in South Africa would become legitimate targets for attack. Understandably irritated, she replied that this showed what a typical terrorist organisation the ANC was.

While a determined opponent of apartheid, Thatcher had never been an admirer of the ANC, given that the 'armed struggle' had been extended to civilian targets and included the necklacing of 'collaborators', and that the organisation was committed to nationalisation of much of the economy. Moreover, she had not failed to notice that, despite the SACP's lack of any mass support, two thirds of the ANC's politburo were members of the SACP. Nor did she believe for a moment that they were in a position to 'seize power'. Nevertheless, she had been persuaded that the ANC had nationwide support and there could be no solution without them.

On her return to London, I telephoned the Prime Minister's Private Secretary, Charles Powell, to say that I understood why she had reacted as she had to a stupidly provocative statement by the ANC representative, who had been speaking on his own behalf. But as he well knew, through the programmes we were organising in the townships, we were in touch with much of the internal leadership of the ANC, while a colleague in Lusaka was in daily touch with the ANC leadership there. Downing Street agreed that of course these contacts must continue. This was confirmed also to Lynda Chalker, Minister of State in the Foreign Office, with the proviso that it should be our objective to get the ANC to agree to a suspension of violence.

At the end of October, I was asked to pass a simple message from the Prime Minister to PW Botha. This was that she had refrained from putting pressure on him, but if he did nothing he would make things difficult for everyone, including him. A few days later, on 5 November, there was a modest step forward, with the release from prison of the long-term Robben Islander and hardline Marxist, Govan Mbeki, father of Thabo. In reporting this, I warned the Prime Minister that the release of Mandela was as remote as ever.

November 1987

Meeting with another senior member of the government, the courteous and erudite Gerrit Viljoen, De Lange's predecessor as head of the Broederbond. His scholarly accomplishments included first-class honours in Classics from King's College, Cambridge. Asked what I wanted to talk about, I said that it was the resettlement of the Magopa people, victims of a forced removal from the Ventersdorp district in 1983. Viljoen put his head in his hands. 'Oh no,' he said, 'I have just had the most dreadful hour with Mrs Suzman about the Magopas and now there's you!' In the event, a partial resettlement was agreed for the Magopas. I had an equally friendly meeting with his cabinet colleague, Dawie de Villiers, former captain of the Springbok rugby team, who also appeared firmly in the ranks of the *verligte*s.

I kept telling South African audiences in Johannesburg and Cape Town that the international campaign for increasing sanctions against them was born not of malevolence, but of frustration at the lack of any visible progress towards any meaningful political rights for the black population. Apartheid was unsustainable; it also was unaffordable. The question was not whether it would disappear, but how protracted its death throes would be, and how much more self-inflicted damage would be done meanwhile. Thanks to Ton Vosloo and the *verligte* editors of *Beeld* and *Die Burger*, Willem Wepener and Ebbe Dommisse, these comments were featured regularly in the Afrikaans press.

At this time the government decided to try to silence one of its most effective critics, the *Weekly Mail* newspaper, which had shown itself to be particularly accurate in exposing many of the murkiest deeds of the security forces. I had befriended its courageous editor, Anton Harber, and other members of the editorial team. The government clearly was hoping that the paper would go to the wall financially before, through the courts, it could get permission to start publishing again. I went to see Anton Harber at the *Weekly Mail* office in Johannesburg to hand over sufficient funding for the paper to be able to survive for the three months or so that looked likely to be necessary to achieve this.

In Pretoria, I attended a party given by a young member of the embassy staff, John Sawers – nowadays head of MI6 – at which Johan Heyns was asked by a group of ANC supporters what he was trying to do. 'I am trying to change the hearts and minds of my people,' replied Heyns. 'That's no use: we want power now,' they asserted. 'But you are not going to get power until I change the hearts and minds of my people,' was Heyns's reply.

December 1987

I arranged for Helen Suzman to meet the Prime Minister. She told Margaret Thatcher that PW Botha had no plans to release Mandela. He wanted to keep the neighbouring countries vulnerable. He had run out of ideas for reform. We had to work on his potential successors.

At the end of the year, I had a discussion with Van Zyl Slabbert.

He believed, as I did, that the idea of a suspension rather than a renunciation of violence was one whose time would come, but not if it were served up from outside. Meanwhile, both sides still thought they could win – the security forces that they could contain the situation and the ANC that they could somehow seize power. Slabbert, Suzman and the influential Stellenbosch academics did not believe that either side could win, but it was still going to take some time for that realisation to sink in. Meanwhile, there was likely to be a period of violent evolution, with the government trying to co-opt black South Africans, without success, and the ANC trying to challenge the state militarily, with equally little success.

CHAPTER IV

———◆———

'If you want to get out of a hole, the first thing to do is to stop digging'

20 January 1988

I delivered a further message from Margaret Thatcher to PW Botha. She said that she had opposed punitive sanctions, though she was totally opposed to apartheid. She had to be able to demonstrate that a policy against further sanctions could yield practical results.

I told PW Botha that the Prime Minister was trying to help South Africa. She could herself be helped or hindered in doing so. We wanted British companies to stay in South Africa, and he could make that easier or more difficult. PW Botha said that he hoped the Prime Minister would visit South Africa to see things for herself. He complained about the sanctions imposed by the US Congress despite what he claimed were his reforms. I warned her that his reply would include considerable argument and self-justification about what already was being done.

February 1988

The South African ambassador delivered to the Prime Minister PW Botha's reply, which was as self-serving as I had predicted, producing an explosion from her. The ambassador was asked to tell the President that his reply contained nothing of substance and failed to address the heart of the matter, which was that apartheid must go. When people had legitimate aspirations, these must be addressed by negotiations. She needed to be able to show progress with political reform; there had to be some hope. She had nothing to show for her battle against more sanctions.

On 24 February, I crossed the road from the British embassy, within the Cape Town parliamentary precinct, to meet a number of National Party MPs on the steps of parliament. I asked about their reaction to the announcement I had just received that the government had banned the UDF. They looked at me in amazement, entirely unaware of the news. PW Botha was to pay a price for this increasing tendency to ignore the parliamentary party, who felt that all important decisions were being taken by the coterie of securocrats around him. The power of the securocrats was exercised through the State Security Council (SSC), operating as an inner cabinet and controlling the National Security Management System (NSMS), whose function was to coordinate the military, intelligence and police response to internal challenges to the regime.

The Prime Minister sent a message to PW Botha deploring the banning of the UDF and the fact that Mandela remained in jail. She had done everything she could to give South Africa time to make political changes. She gave a clear warning that, to resist further sanctions, more progress with political reform was urgently needed. 'I am particularly disappointed that Nelson Mandela remains in prison … if he were to die in prison the damage to South Africa would be enormous.' Her reaction was reported prominently in the South African press. Pik Botha told me that, when he pointed out the external consequences of the government's action, he had simply been overruled.

Archbishop Tutu and the Reverend Allan Boesak organised a meeting in Cape Town's St George's Cathedral, to be followed by a march on parliament to protest against the banning of the UDF. I sent members of the embassy to witness the demonstration. The church leaders explained that, if stopped by the police, the demonstrators should kneel on the pavement and start singing a hymn. With these instructions they set off. As they rounded the corner towards the parliament building, the demonstrators ran into the riot police, led by the redoubtable Major Dolf Odendaal. Archbishop Tutu and Allan Boesak fell to their knees, as did the congregation. Unimpressed, Odendaal opened up with water cannon filled with purple dye, following which he arrested Tutu and Boesak, the wife of the Canadian ambassador and the BBC crew filming the incident. They were quickly released and by lunchtime Allan Boesak, never a one for martyrdom, was to be found eating a lobster in the Tuynhuys restaurant nearby. Meanwhile I was deluged with calls from Lambeth Palace urging me to secure his release and that of Desmond Tutu.

I had dinner that evening with FW de Klerk and Johann Rupert at the Mount Nelson Hotel. Johann Rupert, an outspoken advocate of reform who had been threatened by Magnus Malan if he did not mend his ways, said that he had been discussing a potential investment in South Africa when, on turning on his television, he had discovered the Minister of Law and Order, Adriaan Vlok, stating that the country was on the verge of revolution and that, therefore, the UDF must be banned. He told De Klerk what would happen to the country and its economy if the security junta who were running it continued to behave in this way. I described what had happened at the demonstration we had witnessed earlier in the day. De Klerk made clear, with surprising frankness, that he had not been consulted, and that, if he had been in charge, affairs would have been conducted in a very different way.

March 1988

I saw Neil van Heerden to warn of the potential consequences of the South African ambassador at the United Nations seeking to curry favour with his President, telling the world to 'do its damnedest'.

At the beginning of March, I arranged for Enos Mabuza, the Prime Minister of Kangwane homeland, near the Mozambique border, to meet the Prime Minister. Mabuza, like Buthelezi, had rejected 'independence' for his territory – which, in this case, would have involved incorporation into Swaziland – thereafter being harassed by the security forces. I had visited Kangwane a couple of times to show support for Mabuza and to provide some help in dealing with the flood of Mozambican refugees. For this I received a message of thanks from the ANC in Lusaka. The Prime Minister told him that she understood that he could not negotiate with the South African government so long as Mandela remained in jail.

PW Botha replied to the Prime Minister's message about the

banning of the UDF that they held different views on the reality of South Africa. She was simply ill-informed.

8 March 1988

Further meeting with PW Botha. Pik Botha had asked me if I could not do something to calm the President down. He was worried about the state he was in; his right hand was shaking. The meeting, once again, was tête-à-tête. PW Botha said that Mandela could not be released unless he renounced violence. Otherwise he would have to be arrested on the next day. I said that Mandela's death in prison would do enormous damage. PW Botha had said of the Afrikaner hero General Christiaan de Wet that the indefinite imprisonment of leaders could unleash great emotional forces. Exactly the same was true of Mandela.

PW Botha said that he had made reforms, but the West had let him down, especially the United States. Following the passage of sanctions legislation by the US Congress, the United States had lost all influence in South Africa. I said that Margaret Thatcher had fought many battles to avoid the total isolation of South Africa, but that South Africa kept contributing to its own isolation. Account needed to be taken of her views.

14 and 15 March 1988

I was informed by the Department of Justice that the appeal for clemency by the Sharpeville Six, who had been convicted of the murder of the deputy mayor of Sharpeville, had been turned down by PW Botha. They were due to be executed on 18 March and the preparations for the execution were under way at the prison. On the following day, I arranged for Desmond Tutu to speak to the Prime Minister. He asked her to 'use her considerable influence with PW Botha'. She said that I was being asked to make her views extremely clear to the South African government. Desmond Tutu saw PW Botha on 16 March, only to be berated for leading demonstrations against the regime.

I already had appealed to Anton Rupert to write a letter to PW Botha about the Six. He did so, only to receive a characteristically brutish reply. I contacted Helen Suzman to say that I was planning to see PW Botha before the executions, and so, I knew, was the leader of her party, Colin Eglin. I asked her, in these pretty desperate circumstances, to give up the ban she had imposed on any dealings by her with Botha apart from her attacks on him in parliament. I got in touch with Johan Heyns, who promised me that we would all go separately to see PW Botha to ask for clemency and tell him of the likely consequences if it were to be denied.

16 March 1988

In the meeting with her and Colin Eglin, at the suggestion of her friend Professor David Welsh of the University of Cape Town, Helen Suzman reminded PW Botha of a speech by his former party leader, DF Malan, during the Second World War, when he pleaded for clemency for two Afrikaners sentenced to death for bombing a post office to sabotage the war effort. It was characteristic of Helen Suzman, in dealing with her worst enemy, to find a line of argument most difficult for him to reject. Nor could he afford, on this occasion, to ignore the views of the head of the Dutch Reformed Church or those, which I had made crystal clear to him, of Mrs Thatcher.

17 March 1988

At the eleventh hour, the President announced that the cases would be submitted again to be reviewed by a panel of judges from the Supreme Court. The *Weekly Mail* commented that the Six had a lot to thank us – and Margaret Thatcher – for.

The saga of the Sharpeville Six was not yet quite over, as the review process dragged on. Margaret Thatcher saw Joyce Mokhesi, sister of one of the accused (Francis Mokhesi), to assure her that we were continuing our campaign for clemency, which I did in a further meeting with Kobie Coetsee. Having delivered the usual warning about foreign interference, Coetsee acknowledged that the Prime Minister's intervention had been crucial in helping to get them off death row. In November, the Appeal Court judges rejected the appeal of the Six for a retrial, but PW Botha forthwith commuted the death sentences on them to periods of imprisonment.

April 1988

At this time there occurred an episode that made clear the nature of the regime. The US press had reported that a South African general had admitted to an American diplomat that the SADF had been responsible for a raid on Maputo. The South African military were convinced that the diplomat in question was Bob Frasure, a friend of mine in the US embassy (he was later to be tragically killed in an accident in Bosnia). They proceeded to engage in a Soviet-style campaign of harassment against Frasure and his family. He was ostentatiously followed everywhere; on one occasion his car was forced off the road. The telephone lines were cut at his home at night. The windows of his house were broken, also at night. His wife was terrorised, and Frasure had to be withdrawn by the State Department. Why they permitted this to happen without denouncing publicly what had occurred was something I was never able to understand.

Having been invited to address the annual meeting in Johannesburg of the Urban Foundation, a non-profit organisation founded in 1977 by South African business leaders, I decided that it was time to deliver a decidedly undiplomatic speech, of a kind that would have got me thrown out of any other African country. In the 1960s, I pointed out, South Africa had been able to maintain apartheid and still have economic growth. That was not possible any longer. South Africa was approaching a further turning point in its relations with the outside world. 'We do not believe in your isolation, but we cannot prevent you isolating yourselves ... If you want to get out of a hole, the first thing to do is to stop digging.' Unless South Africa repealed the remaining apartheid laws, they would get no further support from us.

This was splashed all over the South African press. Pik Botha complained to me formally about the speech, as he was bound to do, while also telling me that he agreed with it. Several other members of the government told me that they agreed, without bothering to complain.

May 1988

PW Botha, meanwhile, was fulminating against the English-speaking universities, which he regarded as hotbeds of subversion. He was threatening to introduce a bill in parliament to curtail the political activities of both students and staff. The vice chancellors of the universities appealed for help, and Helen Suzman and I went separately to see De Klerk, as the Minister of Education, about this. We were told that he had no intention of pushing through such a bill in the current parliamentary session. We seemed to have found one minister who was prepared to stand up to his irascible President.

CHAPTER V

---·—·—·---

'The IRA have the vote, the ANC do not'

9 June 1988

Meeting with the Prime Minister in London. I was asked to tell PW Botha and the other members of the South African government of the growing difficulties South Africa would face unless progress was made towards the release of Mandela, a settlement in Namibia, normalisation with Mozambique and steps to dismantle the remaining apartheid laws. Above all, Margaret Thatcher insisted on the release of Mandela. I told her that no reliance whatever could be placed on PW Botha, but that he was becoming increasingly isolated.

July 1988

I told Pik Botha that, if he wanted us to be able to exert any influence on an incoming US administration, there would have to be progress on Namibia and Mandela. He said that he agreed, as did Kobie Coetsee, but the security chiefs were still arguing that with Mandela's release the situation would be out of control. I protested about draft legislation seeking to ban foreign funding for civic organisations in South Africa. He said that this would be modified. He claimed that support for Renamo was being cut off.

I delivered a reply to Dr Jannie Roux, secretary-general to the President, about his further complaints about the ANC office and visits to London by Ronnie Kasrils, head of intelligence for MK, and Joe Slovo, general secretary of the SACP and also chief of staff of MK. We would not, I said, permit any office in the UK to be used for the purpose of preparing violent acts abroad. If the South Africans had any evidence to that effect, they would need to present it to us.

Dr Roux and the President's security advisor, General Pieter van der Westhuizen, the two officials closest to PW Botha, inspired as little confidence as the President did himself, with Dr Roux telling me that he regarded Robben Island as the kind of place where he too might end up some day, with others like him, if the ANC came to power. He and his master regarded majority rule as solving our problems but not theirs.

The Prime Minister saw Buthelezi and Laurens van der Post at 10 Downing Street. She agreed that he could not be expected to negotiate with the government with Mandela still in jail, a point she emphasised in a further message to PW Botha. She was, she said, deeply concerned that Mandela remained in prison after twenty-six years. If he died in prison, the consequences would be disastrous.

August 1988

The Prime Minister's message served only to produce a long argumentative reply from PW Botha, which she found 'far from helpful', claiming that Buthelezi was uncooperative and that Kasrils had been allowed to visit London again even though MK had declared that it would be targeting 'soft', i.e. civilian, targets.

I asked the Prime Minister to meet Willem Wepener, the editor of *Beeld*, one of the two leading Afrikaans newspapers. He had published an editorial calling for the release of Mandela, only to be denounced publicly by PW Botha. In response, Wepener had refused to give way, stating that 'we are not the South African Broadcasting Corporation, at any rate not yet!'

Gerhard de Kock told me about a lunch he had arranged at the Reserve Bank for the senior hierarchy of the South African Police. He had found, to his amazement, that they were convinced that, if further unrest broke out, it could easily be quelled by arresting a few thousand more people. They had no conception of the economic consequences of their actions. South Africa could 'limp along' like this, but there would be no chance of raising living standards.

I was invited to join Van Heerden and Barend du Plessis on a visit to a game camp in the Okavango Delta in Botswana. Both told me that they agreed with De Kock. Both wanted to see a settlement in Namibia if the Cubans really would withdraw. I stressed our concern that Mandela had been hospitalised again, this time for tuberculosis. Both said that the government supported his release, but PW Botha listened only to the security chiefs. I reported to London that there was currently a great deal of unhappiness among key figures in the Afrikaner establishment about PW Botha and the fix the government had got itself into with the failure of its efforts to co-opt any worthwhile black leaders.

September 1988

Meeting with Kobie Coetsee about Mandela. Coetsee said that he was making good progress and would soon be able to leave the clinic. PW Botha had agreed that he should not be sent back to Pollsmoor prison. I said that we welcomed the humane way in which Mandela was being treated, as he had himself confirmed to Helen Suzman, but what was needed was to release him. Coetsee responded that the government needed some guarantee that he would behave responsibly. I said that his continued presence in prison was, quite simply, a time bomb of the government's own making.

I had got to know Coetsee well enough to know that he was strongly in favour of Mandela's release. A courteous and civilised man, he had formed a close relationship with his prisoner, which was to grow still closer over the next eighteen months. (Following the 1994 elections, Mandela ensured that Coetsee became Speaker of the upper house of the new South African parliament.)

Helen Suzman told me that, when she saw Mandela at the Constantiaberg Clinic, he said that he would like to do something to help normalise the situation in South Africa. But when he was released, after twenty-six years, he could not be expected to remain 'with his arms folded'.

October 1988

I informed Buthelezi that we had told Thabo Mbeki of his desire to end the violence between Inkatha and ANC supporters in Natal. I spoke also to Buthelezi's deputy, Oscar Dhlomo, to encourage his efforts to reduce the violence through his contacts with the labour unions and the UDF. Inkatha had its warlords, but so did the ANC. The government had released from jail on medical grounds the hardline SACP member Harry Gwala, who was quickly to establish himself as the leading ANC warlord in Natal and to take the lead in opposing any understanding with Inkatha. Asked by a journalist on one occasion about his 'armies of the night', Gwala's reply was: 'What about my armies of the day?'

November 1988

According to his foreign policy advisor, Anatoly Chernyaev, Mikhail Gorbachev had admitted to the Soviet Politburo that Margaret Thatcher had exposed the contradiction between domestic reform and the continuance of old-style Soviet foreign policy, which had become unaffordable anyway.[13] At a time of increasing domestic hardship, expensive support for Soviet-backed regimes in Africa, such as Angola, Ethiopia and Mozambique, had become increasingly unpopular in Russia. Gorbachev had by then decided to withdraw Soviet forces from Afghanistan, where they had been waging a costly war since the end of 1979.

Niel Barnard, head of the National Intelligence Service (NIS), showed himself to be more aware than the police and army generals of the extent to which Soviet policy really had changed. Namibia and the conflict in Angola had become an unacceptable financial drain for South Africa. Mandela, he agreed, could not be allowed to die in jail. PW Botha was old-fashioned and out of touch.

10 November

Meeting with Adriaan Vlok, Minister of Law and Order. He said that he could not recommend Mandela's unconditional release. As he appeared to be hinting at some form of house arrest, I said that Mandela's release would be of great value only if it led into negotiations on a new constitution. It would be no use continuing to submit him to all sorts of restrictions.

I pressed for the release of a number of detainees, including the journalist Zwelakhe Sisulu. I warned him against following the advice of the head of the security police, General Basie Smit, who was calling for many more organisations to be banned.

The government announced that Mandela was to be transferred to 'suitable, comfortable and secure living accommodation'. In fact, he was transferred the following month to a warden's cottage in the grounds of the Victor Verster prison, near Paarl. While the conditions of his imprisonment had been transformed, he remained every bit as much a prisoner as before.

Beeld published the Prime Minister's interview with Willem Wepener, under a banner heading quoting her as saying that 'The IRA have the vote, the ANC do not'. She was, she said, against all forms of terrorism, but the ANC was an important factor in South African politics. The question was how to get them to give up violence. That would entail a suspension of violence on all sides.

December 1988

To increase the pressure on PW Botha, Margaret Thatcher had been seeking to persuade Chancellor Helmut Kohl of West Germany to agree to a joint approach to the South African President. A speaking note was agreed, covering the need to implement the agreement provisionally reached on Namibia (see page 87) but, above all, to release Nelson Mandela and engage in negotiations on a new constitution. The envoy chosen for this joint mission was the Swiss banker Fritz Leutwiler, who in 1985, when the international banks refused to extend further credit to South Africa, had helped the South Africans (and their creditors) by agreeing a phased schedule for the repayment of South Africa's debts, thereby avoiding a default.

The Prime Minister saw Leutwiler in London. She told him that she could not go on indefinitely exerting her influence against further sanctions unless she could show results. Leutwiler said that he intended to tell PW Botha that in default of further reforms he would lose South Africa's few remaining friends. But Leutwiler was not hopeful of results.

12 December 1988

Leutwiler called on me in Pretoria to say that he had handed over the joint UK-German message to PW Botha. It had been a tense and difficult meeting. PW Botha was bitter and emotional. Correctly identifying Margaret Thatcher as the main author of this *démarche*, he felt that she was being unfair. She was constantly pressurising the South African government, and so was I. We were not going to get them to Lancaster House. He had argued that Mandela was 'practically a free man', living in a nice house with a swimming pool. He had refused to agree to be sent to the Transkei. If he were released, he might be killed and the South African government would be blamed.

68

He would be likely to go to Soweto and address a crowd of a hundred thousand people. There would be unrest and the government would have to arrest him again. If he as President were to appear on television and say that Mandela was being released, he would have to step down on the same day.

Shifting tack, Botha suggested that the government possibly might release Mandela if Western countries would then lift sanctions. Leutwiler said that he was not there to bargain. The President clearly did not understand that Western governments could not simply instruct the banks to resume lending to South Africa. He had suggested, ridiculously, that South Africa did not have political prisoners, and had bridled at any mention of Buthelezi.

Leutwiler's conclusion was that the President was a bitter old man, with a very unhealthy atmosphere around him. Pik Botha and Barend du Plessis both had agreed with the message that was being delivered, but neither had said a word in the meeting, except to agree with the President.

Leutwiler reported subsequently to the Prime Minister that the last-ditch atmosphere around PW Botha was like that which must have prevailed around Hitler in his bunker.

CHAPTER VI

——◆——

'I realise you want to see a new impetus for change'

January 1989

While preparing for the opening of the new parliamentary session, PW Botha suffered a stroke. The Prime Minister sent him a polite message saying that she was sorry to hear that he had been suddenly taken ill. Chris Heunis was appointed Acting President. I reported that this did not mean that he was likely to succeed PW Botha. De Klerk was likely to be the successor. I added that, in this highly autocratic system, the President's illness was likely to create a prolonged period of uncertainty. I forecast that he would still try to hang on grimly.

A week later, I reported that most of his cabinet hoped PW Botha would retire, but doubted he would do so. He was tired, confused and not capable of taking decisions for the time being. He would have to face an election within a year. His most likely successor, FW de Klerk, was friendly, approachable, personally impressive, much calmer and more pragmatic, but preoccupied with the right-wing threat in the Transvaal. He feared that immediate repeal of the Group Areas Act could cost him his own seat in parliament. But he had strong views on the need for firm civilian control over the military.

Rudolph Agnew of Consolidated Goldfields reported to Charles Powell at 10 Downing Street on the secret talks at Mells Park between a small group of Afrikaners led by Professor Willie Esterhuyse of Stellenbosch University and Thabo Mbeki and his colleagues in the ANC. Esterhuyse was believed by the Mells Park organisers to be a senior advisor to PW Botha, which, unfortunately, was not the case. But, as he told Mbeki, he was reporting back to senior members of the NIS. Esterhuyse himself told me about these contacts in February. I told him that meetings of this kind with the ANC were welcomed by us. We knew that he had established a good rapport with Mbeki. These were emphatically not negotiations, but they had opened up a useful channel of communication with the ANC.

The Prime Minister attended a dinner in London with Jan Steyn, head of the Urban Foundation, Anton Rupert and the heads of Rio Tinto, BP and Shell. I warned that they would tell her that they had little influence on the South African government, but Anton Rupert was a friend of De Klerk and could have an important influence on him.

2 February 1989

De Klerk was elected by the National Party members of parliament to replace PW Botha as leader of the National Party, though Botha intended to cling on to his position as President. De Klerk defeated Barend du Plessis by sixty-nine votes to sixty-one, with several of the *verligte* National Party MPs voting for the finance minister, who was thought also to have the support of PW Botha, not because the President had suddenly become a reformist, but because Barend had less of an independent power base than De Klerk.

I was on good terms with both the contestants, but was glad of the outcome, as I had been impressed by De Klerk's strength of character, which was going to be badly needed in the period ahead. He was not PW Botha's favourite and would want to take over from him sooner rather than later. I also thought it easier for hawks than doves to make peace, once they were decided to do so. De Klerk was not Gorbachev, I reported, but we had a good relationship with him.

At the opening of parliament, De Klerk had asked Helen Suzman why he was regarded as *verkramp*. 'Because you never make a *verligte* speech', was her reply. De Klerk proceeded, in his first statement as head of the National Party, to make a very *verligte* speech indeed, declaring that the aim must be to realise full civil rights for all South Africans and a democratic system in which no community was dominated by another or felt itself to be threatened or excluded.

3 February 1989

I called on De Klerk in his office in parliament. He had said that he would be glad to see me at any time. There was going to be a difficult period ahead. Most of the ministers and National Party MPs hoped that the President would stand down. I said that PW Botha's staff were telling me that he would not do so. He was resentful and suspicious of De Klerk. I passed on to De Klerk an invitation from the Prime Minister to an early meeting with her.

Pik Botha, meanwhile, had been probing the government in London as to whether sanctions would be lifted if Mandela were released. The Prime Minister agreed that sanctions should be lifted only if Mandela's release led into negotiations on a new constitution.

17 February 1989

Further meeting with FW de Klerk. He told me that he did not know how things were going to work out with PW Botha. Rather than resigning, the President might well try to hold on for some time. He doubted if this could continue for many months – there had to be an election – but De Klerk could not go to London in the near term. He would do so later in the year. He had a high regard for the Prime Minister, and regarded the ties with Britain as the most important relationship South Africa had, as US policy was hamstrung by Congress. He had ideas about what needed to be done and plenty of authority within the party, but he was not yet in the driving seat. He realised that we wanted to see a new impetus for change.

I said that, if he was able to take South Africa in a different direction, we would try to help him. But if the security police and military intelligence were allowed to continue their activities, including murder squads, unchecked, there was no way any of us were going to be able to help South Africa. We had evidence that, despite all the disclaimers, South African military intelligence were continuing to support Renamo in Mozambique. Other elements of the security forces were strongly suspected of murdering opponents of the regime.

De Klerk told me that he heard what I was saying. He had never been involved in authorising these activities and was determined to

73

deal with them. But, he added carefully, as I would understand, he would have to deal with the security forces with a velvet glove.

De Klerk agreed on the importance of implementing the agreement leading to the independence of Namibia and not backtracking on any part of it. I said that the Prime Minister did not understand the government's failure to engage more seriously with Buthelezi on constitutional issues. The key issue, however, was the release of Mandela. De Klerk said that he was not security-dominated in his thinking. But the situation had to be dealt with in a way that did not advance the cause of a revolution. I said that Mandela's continued detention was being exploited by people who wanted to do just that. South Africa was now heading for an election, but Mandela's release could not indefinitely be deferred.

23 February 1989
Meeting with Barend du Plessis to tell him that the Prime Minister would like to see him when he was in London in April. He had been explaining to his cabinet colleagues that South Africa's debt-repayment problem constrained economic growth to well below the level needed to provide for a population currently increasing by three quarters of a million people per year. I said that, if Mandela died in prison, the result would be an internal explosion and near-total isolation. When I raised this with General Malan or the police chiefs, they said that releasing Mandela would give a new impetus to revolution. But I did not believe that they had any understanding of the economic consequences of not releasing him. A resumption of investment would happen only if Western banks and governments believed that South Africa had more convincing plans for its own future.

March 1989

Following the assassination of Dulcie September, the ANC representative in Paris, in March 1988, we became concerned about the possibility of an attack on ANC personnel in London. The Prime Minister
decreed that we must give the South African government the clearest
possible warning that any such action would attract a strong reaction
from us, which I duly relayed to Van Heerden and the Presidency. This
included telling them that we had received information that South
African military agents were planning such action and this must be
terminated immediately.

I reported that, to the dismay of his ministers, PW Botha was planning to return to his office. De Klerk was continuing to make reformist
statements and the cabinet had rallied behind him. PW Botha was
declining to set a date for an early election, causing a head-on clash
with De Klerk, who also was being supported by the Afrikaans press,
with Wepener and *Die Burger* calling publicly on the President to go.
Even Botha's closest allies were telling me that he would have to stand
down.

As my friend Kobus Meiring had been appointed Administrator
of the Cape – the senior official of the province – I asked him to
promise at last to open the magnificent beaches to South Africans of
all races. Kobus, whose own apartment at the Strand was on a still-
segregated beach, needed no persuasion to do so.

It now became possible to discuss with members of the government all the issues that had been forbidden territory for so long, as they
were terrified of their leader. I was able to establish a regular pattern
of meetings with De Klerk, who had convinced me of his intention to

make major changes. De Klerk's friends were not the security chiefs, but the business community of Johannesburg, and precisely those leading Afrikaners who had felt alienated under PW Botha.

Gerhard de Kock by this time was dying of cancer. He was a golf-playing friend of De Klerk's, and was determined to warn the new leader of the National Party what would happen to South Africa if the capital outflow continued. De Kock spent the last months of his life convincing his friend that only disaster could result from continuing on this course.

CHAPTER VII

———❖———

'The whole world will be against you – led by me!'

In my first meeting with him, I told PW Botha that I did not know whether, in my time as ambassador, I would see the end of all the remaining apartheid legislation. But I did hope to see a solution at last to the long-standing problem of independence for Namibia.

Shortly afterwards, I made the first of a series of visits to Namibia, still firmly under South African control. This wild and beautiful territory is a place to which it is easy to form a strong attachment. Most of the country is semi-desert, with vast farms able to support only a few animals. The Skeleton Coast and Etosha Pan are two of the world's great nature reserves. The only easily cultivable land is in the Kunene Valley in the north, inhabited by the Ovambo people, where the war between South African forces and Swapo guerrillas was at its worst.

Namibia had been colonised by the Germans at the tail end of the nineteenth-century 'scramble for Africa', and they had named it South West Africa. The two main streets of the tiny capital, Windhoek, were named Kaiser Wilhelmstrasse and Goeringstrasse – the latter a reference to Hermann Goering's father, Heinrich, the first governor of South West Africa. At the outbreak of the First World War, at Britain's request, South Africa had invaded and seized the colony. On the coast, populated mainly by flamingos, lay the Baltic-style village of Swakopmund with, in the cemetery, the graves of Germans killed in that long-forgotten conflict. In the north, there were plenty more graves in evidence, of more recent origin.

I went to South Africa determined to combine my efforts with those of my friend Dr Chester Crocker, Assistant Secretary of State for Africa under President Ronald Reagan, to achieve an end to the protracted war in the territory. Chet Crocker at the time was being severely criticised by the European foreign ministries, including our own, for linking South African withdrawal from Namibia to the withdrawal of the thirty thousand Cuban troops in Angola. This was a good example of the bizarre positions diplomats from time to time get themselves into. Personally I thought the linkage was entirely justified. For it was, in any event, desirable to get the Cubans out of Angola and I did not see how, otherwise, we were going to persuade the South Africans to withdraw from Namibia.

October 1987

The MPLA government in Angola, led by President Eduardo dos Santos, launched a major offensive designed finally to crush Jonas Savimbi's Unita guerrillas in their main redoubt in southeastern Angola. The attack was meticulously planned by the Angolan army's Soviet military advisors. As the massive force they assembled advanced south and east from the provincial capital of Cuito Cuanavale towards Savimbi's headquarters at Jamba, they were ambushed by South African forces on the Lomba River. The leading Angolan brigade was decimated. The rest of the Angolan force withdrew in confusion to Cuito Cuanavale, suffering further losses as it did so. Savimbi claimed a great victory.

The South Africans had been operating in Angola ever since 1975, when Henry Kissinger encouraged them to intervene to prevent the Communist-backed MPLA from seizing the capital, Luanda. When that venture failed, the main South African forces withdrew. Having fallen back to the Namibian border, they soon discovered that the most effective way to disrupt infiltration by Swapo guerrillas into northern Namibia was by intercepting them in southern Angola. This was done through the use of small but determined special forces units, South African-led but with Bushman trackers. Angolan opponents of the regime in Luanda were organised into the Portuguese-speaking 32 Battalion, which specialised in cross-border operations. At the same time, the SADF continued the supply of weaponry and fuel to Unita and sought to coordinate military operations with them. As necessary, these were supported by South African mechanised units. By these tactics, and through the exercise of local air superiority, over the next fourteen years the South Africans turned much of southern Angola into a free-fire zone.

The South African foreign ministry continued to issue strenuous denials that South Africa was involved in any way in the fighting in Angola. Pik Botha was particularly eloquent on this subject. South African military units, operating deep inside Angola or Mozambique, used to listen on their radios with amusement to their government's indignant denials. Nor did Colonel Jan Breytenbach, the 32 Battalion commander, and his colleagues on the border very often bother to seek political approval for their operations. These received all the support they required from the South African military command. As PW Botha and his colleagues became frequent visitors to Savimbi's South African-supplied headquarters in Jamba, they knew perfectly well the extent of these cross-border incursions.

Stopping the massive Soviet- and Cuban-backed advance in October 1987 required some heroic actions by 32 Battalion and the other heavily outnumbered South African forces involved. The South African force never exceeded a brigade in size, and much of its success rested on superior mobility and tactics. The battle was won by concentrated artillery fire and air strikes on Angolan tank formations. Huge quantities of Soviet equipment were destroyed or captured. As always, the public credit for the victory was awarded to Unita, despite Jan Breytenbach's low regard for their fighting qualities. The Soviet military advisors took an even dimmer view of the performance of their Angolan allies.

November 1987

Visiting Namibia, I was briefed by a half-mad South African colonel on the battle of the Lomba River, which was indeed an impressive military exploit. On the struggle against Swapo in Namibia, he took the view that victory was certain – but for the efforts of the enemy within. When I inquired who the enemy within were, he replied: 'The churches, the trade unions and the teachers.'

After their victory on the Lomba River, the South African forces, operating hundreds of kilometres inside Angola, overreached themselves. It never was the intention of General Jannie Geldenhuys, head of the SADF, that they should try to take and hold Cuito Cuanavale. As, however, they attempted to eliminate the Angolan bridgehead on the eastern bank of the Cuito River, they found themselves up against entrenched Cuban armour and heavy artillery fire. The South African attempt to eliminate the bridgehead was beaten off and a battle of attrition ensued.

Stung by the failure of their great offensive, the Cuban commanders at last came up with an effective military response. Hitherto, they had kept their forces well back from the Namibian border and away from South African attacks on infiltrating Swapo guerrillas. Cuban forces in the western sector now were reinforced and instructed to move south, bringing them much closer to the border. Their tank formations posed a serious threat to the lightly armed South African reconnaissance forces, hitherto used to operating with impunity in the area. The South Africans had to wonder whether the Cuban tanks might seek to cross the border, where there was not enough South African armour to oppose them. For both sides, the war had entered a new and potentially much more dangerous phase, raising the possibility of a direct South Africa/Cuba confrontation.

* * *

In international affairs, some problems are easier to tackle when they have reached the point of crisis than when they are merely heading there. While acknowledging the skill their forces had shown in the battle on the Lomba River, I asked the South Africans whether they did not think they were in danger of overreaching themselves. Johan Heyns inquired publicly whether it made sense to have men 'defending South Africa' two hundred miles inside Angola. The South Africans had suffered significant casualties; theirs was a citizen army, and several of those killed were conscripts. Attending a dinner in Johannesburg at the house of a National Party MP, I found that virtually everyone there agreed with Professor Heyns – including the MP.

South Africa was fortunate at this juncture in having Neil van Heerden at the head of its foreign ministry. We spent many hours together discussing ways to breathe fresh life into the Namibia negotiations. The South Africans hitherto had never really been prepared to contemplate giving up Namibia. Now that the stakes had risen, I argued, it was in their interests to consider doing so – provided agreement could be reached on a credible programme for Cuban withdrawal from Angola.

Pik Botha was at the time, along with West Germany's Hans-Dietrich Genscher, the world's longest-serving foreign minister, and was a veteran of countless unsuccessful Namibia negotiations. The South Africans had chosen to install Dirk Mudge and his colleagues in the pro-South African Democratic Turnhalle Alliance as the government in Windhoek, but all real power still rested with the military, led by General Georg Meiring, and the South African Administrator, Louis Pienaar. Mudge privately showed himself well aware that Swapo, probably, had more support than he did, and near universal support among the Ovambo. Pienaar, though deeply conservative,

became a personal friend and I was convinced that he would cooper-
ate in implementing a settlement if his government's policy changed.

Pik Botha kept telling me that South African policy *was* about
to change. But he had been saying that for years. Botha was one of
the great characters of South African politics. Built like a buffalo, he
would sit in his shirtsleeves, a thick black lock of hair falling across his
face, complaining about the world's supposed injustice towards South
Africa. Sessions with him were always entertaining, but never short.
An accomplished actor, as he needed to be given the policies he tried
with brio to defend, he usually began with a tremendous display of
temperament, amid threats to expel some offending journalist or, on
one occasion, the German ambassador! Never hesitating to perjure
himself in public, he was devastatingly frank in private, not least about
his colleagues. Whatever his faults, which were not small ones, I always
found him an ally in arguing with his President and the security forces
for a Namibia settlement and for internal reform. I believed him when
he told me that he felt the time at last had come when we really could
hope to achieve a solution, if the Cubans were prepared to withdraw.

The moving spirit behind the Namibia negotiations was the US
envoy, Chester Crocker. He was continuing indefatigably to work on
the Russians and Cubans, and he too was beginning to sense a break-
through. For the war in Angola was becoming unpopular in Cuba.
The Russians, increasingly disillusioned, were beginning to contemplate cutting their losses in Africa. At around this time Eduard
Shevardnadze, Gorbachev's foreign minister, making a voyage of dis-
covery to the region, astounded a number of African governments by
telling them that, in future, Russia's relations with them were going

to be conducted on the basis of cost-benefit analysis! To my surprise, I started receiving notes from Boris Asoyan, the deputy chief of the Department of African Countries at the Soviet foreign ministry and the *de facto* Soviet envoy in southern Africa, approving of my public statements that what South Africa needed was not more sanctions or armed struggle, but a negotiated outcome.

January 1988

The Angolans for the first time indicated a willingness to agree in principle to eventual Cuban withdrawal. This would be phased over four years. The South Africans remained deeply sceptical. In May, we made available a venue in London for the first in a new series of negotiations, led by Crocker, between the South Africans, Cubans and Angolans. In June the discussions resumed in Cairo, this time with Pik Botha and General Malan conducting some well-publicised tourism on camels by the Pyramids.

Further meetings followed at various venues. British involvement was indirect but important, for the Americans had no embassy in Luanda. Our ambassador to Angola, Patrick Fairweather, served as the indispensable channel of communications for the Americans, and was able to influence the Angolan replies. Following the imposition by Congress of general sanctions against South Africa, in 1986, there had been a near-breakdown of relations between the Reagan administration and the South African government. So we also had to do a good deal of the heavy lifting in Pretoria, not only with Pik Botha and Van Heerden, but also with other members of the South African government. On 9 May the Prime Minister sent a message to

PW Botha saying: 'It would be a major prize to secure the withdrawal of Cuban troops from Angola and an internationally accepted settlement in Namibia.'

June 1988

Neil van Heerden told me that there had been a sea change in the South African attitude. The political leadership felt that the military had indeed overreached themselves and that further casualties around Cuito Cuanavale were unacceptable. The South Africans also had begun to realise that a profound change really was taking place in Soviet policy.

South African and Cuban minds were concentrated by incidents on the battlefield. As Cuban forces by now were close up against the Namibian border near the Calueque hydroelectric power station on the Kunene River, the South Africans engaged a Cuban column north of the border, inflicting heavy casualties. In retaliation Cuban MiGs bombed the dam and the pumping station, which was controlled by the South Africans, eleven of whom were killed. Although there had been isolated incidents in the air, these were the first major direct clashes between Cuban and South African forces. Having tasted blood, some of it their own, both sides drew back from further exploits of this kind.

July/August 1988

Van Heerden and Pik Botha were working hard for a settlement. To convince PW Botha and the South African military, they needed to be able to persuade them that Cuban withdrawal really was assured.

85

At a meeting in New York the leader of the Cuban delegation, Carlos Aldana, told Van Heerden that they were interested in a 'peace without losers'. Going further than any European foreign ministry was prepared to do, Aldana added that linkage (of Namibian independence to Cuban troop withdrawal) 'exists and its existence is accepted'. One month later, in Geneva, Van Heerden responded by proposing that the process leading to Namibian independence should be started – once the South Africans were satisfied about the modalities for Cuban withdrawal.

By this stage I was convinced that a Namibia settlement was within our grasp. Neither South Africa nor Cuba had any real desire any longer to bear the escalating costs of the war. By November a schedule had been worked out whereby Cuban forces in southern Angola would withdraw to the north – and then leave. In December, this agreement was signed in New York – a triumph of persistence for Chet Crocker and his team.

But with the election of George Bush senior, Crocker by now was close to leaving the scene. Bush's Secretary of State, James Baker, felt that Crocker had become too much of a liability with the black caucus in Congress. As my experience in Rhodesia led me to suspect that implementing the agreement would be no less difficult than negotiating it, I was dismayed at this news. Crocker told me that Britain was going to have to take on much of the burden of helping to ensure that the agreement was in fact implemented.

*　*　*

1 April 1989

The New York Accords, which ended the war in Angola, opened the way for the implementation of UN Security Council Resolution 435, which contained a plan for a ceasefire and UN-supervised elections in Namibia. A multinational force, the United Nations Transitional Assistance Group (Untag), was formed to supervise the elections, which were scheduled for November.

Margaret Thatcher was due to make a visit to Nigeria, Zimbabwe and Malawi. I wanted her to end this tour in Namibia, arriving on 1 April – the day on which the UN plan, to which the South Africans had agreed, began to be implemented. But we would not know until the last moment what the situation would be in Windhoek on that day. I went ahead to Windhoek, and it was agreed by Margaret Thatcher that a decision should be taken only as she was about to leave Malawi.

Having talked to the South African Administrator, the UN representatives – the Finnish diplomat (and future President of Finland) Martti Ahtisaari and General Prem Chand, of the Indian army – the British military signals contingent who were providing communications for the UN force and a number of black Namibian friends, I sent a message urging her to come. Foreign Office officials, understandably concerned that the Prime Minister might find herself in a difficult situation, felt that this was a risk not worth taking. As always, she took pleasure in overruling them. The press accompanying Mrs Thatcher on her plane were told only in mid-air that they were heading for Namibia, not Heathrow.

So, as Namibia returned to legality, the prime ministerial VC10 arrived at Windhoek airport. Mrs Thatcher had lunch in their tented camp with the British personnel. The rest of us had fizzy water, but the troops, thoughtfully, had provided Denis Thatcher with an indistinguishable gin and tonic. We then set off for the British-owned Rössing uranium mine, on which Namibia depended for much of its exports. There had been fierce pressures on Rio Tinto to close down the mine, which would have been a disaster for Namibia, as it would have been extremely costly and difficult to open it up again. Instead the company had set an example by developing housing, health, pensions, safety and other standards far superior to those anywhere else in the territory.

As we boarded the plane for Rössing, the first reports were coming in of large-scale Swapo incursions and clashes on the Angolan border. By the time we returned to Windhoek, it was clear that the entire agreement was threatened.

Louis Pienaar reported that large armed Swapo columns, crossing the border contrary to the terms of the ceasefire agreement, had been intercepted by South African forces. This was the situation we had faced in Rhodesia when, immediately following the ceasefire, large numbers of Mugabe's guerrilla forces moved across the Mozambique border into Rhodesia with their weapons. It had been touch and go to dissuade the Rhodesians from attacking them. The South Africans had far more formidable military capabilities, though their forces were restricted to bases under the terms of the ceasefire agreement. Both sides already were behaving as if the agreement was no longer in existence. Martti Ahtisaari, who had joined us at Pienaar's residence, was in an impossibly difficult position. The South Africans were on the verge of withdrawing from the settlement. Mrs Thatcher told Ahtisaari that he must get agreement from the UN Secretary-General, Javier Pérez de Cuéllar, to authorise South African ground forces to stop the Swapo incursions.

The scene shifted to a long and extremely difficult meeting with Pik Botha at the airport. Under pressure from the military in Pretoria, he was adamant that the South Africans would have to take the law into their own hands and call in air strikes against the Swapo columns, whether the UN authorised these or not. Mrs Thatcher said that she had told Ahtisaari that he must get Pérez de Cuéllar to authorise the local South African forces to deal with the incursions, but that, if the South Africans took unilateral action, 'the whole world will be against you – led by me!'

Pik Botha, on this occasion, though highly overwrought, was not play-acting. He and Van Heerden had invested much personal credit in negotiating an honourable way out for South Africa from Namibia. He now had every hawk in the South African security establishment desperate to resume the fight against their foes in Swapo.

I argued fiercely against air strikes. This went on for two hours, until Denis Thatcher mercifully intervened, as the Prime Minister had to board her plane. As I returned to Windhoek, I was told that the UN had accepted the need for action to deal with the incursions and Pik Botha told me the air strikes had been called off. Ground forces and police units were allowed to deploy instead.

Margaret Thatcher boarded her plane reluctantly. She clearly was attracted by the prospect of continuing to conduct the affairs of Namibia. Martti Ahtisaari was heavily criticised for his actions and had shown plenty of political courage in taking them. If he had not done so, the settlement would have been lost. The Prime Minister had some justification for thinking that she had been 'the right person, in the right place, at the right time'.[14]

But it remained to control the military situation. We used our embassy in Luanda, where Patrick Fairweather's successor, James Glaze, was in direct touch with the Angolan chief of staff. He, the Cubans and the Russians did not want the Swapo incursions to continue: they realised what was at stake. So did several of the senior members of the Swapo political leadership, who also were contacted by Glaze. Gradually an uneasy truce was restored.

CHAPTER VIII

'I am happy to request you to pass my very best wishes to the Prime Minister'

On arriving in South Africa, I had grappled with the problem of how to communicate with Nelson Mandela. I did not have to do so for long. In May 1986, Helen Suzman had seen Mandela in Pollsmoor prison. He had told her that he was ready to negotiate with the government and that he wanted to 'normalise conditions' in South Africa. She did not know when she would be permitted to see him again. I asked her, when she did, to tell him that the Prime Minister was intensifying her efforts to help to secure his release.

When she saw Mandela during his treatment at the Constantiaberg Clinic in August 1988, he told her again that he wanted to help change the situation and could not be expected to sit 'with his arms folded' once he was released. Shortly afterwards, to the alarm of the ANC in Lusaka, he wrote a secret memorandum to PW Botha proposing negotiations to find a solution acceptable to all South Africans. I did not know the content of the memorandum, but I did know that

Mandela favoured negotiations and did not believe in the ANC mantra of a 'seizure of power'.

Nor did most of his colleagues in Lusaka. In January 1990, in a speech intended for an internal audience but which, inadvertently, he made in public, the ANC secretary-general, Alfred Nzo, declared that 'We must admit that we do not have the capacity within our country to intensify the armed struggle in any meaningful way'.[15]

13 April 1989

I reported to the Prime Minister that I had received a letter on prison notepaper from Nelson Mandela. Mandela had told one of his lawyers, Hymie Bernardt, to pass on his thanks to me for the work we were doing in the townships, and I had relayed this to London. To my annoyance, this found its way into the British press as a supposed message from him to Mrs Thatcher. Mandela wrote to me that 'If I had wanted to express my views on Mrs Thatcher's work, or on the policy of the British government on any specific matter, I would have preferred to do so in the course of a face to face discussion with you. Meanwhile, I am happy to request you to pass my very best wishes to the Prime Minister.'

I replied to Mandela: 'Thank you for your letter, which I was very glad to receive. The Prime Minister's position is well known. It is that you should be freed and free to express your views. Needless to say, I should be very glad to have a face to face discussion with you. I have been asked to assure you that our efforts will continue to promote the idea of a negotiation in which all parties can participate, in the context of a suspension of violence on all sides.

'I have, as you requested, passed your best wishes to my Prime Minister. Mrs Thatcher has asked me to send you her best wishes and to say that she looks forward to the day when she is able to discuss these matters with you herself, as she would very much wish to do.'

24 April 1989

In a meeting with Barend du Plessis before his departure for London, I said that the real danger for South Africa was not revolution, but a progressive and worsening economic haemorrhage. The new government would have the chance to change the course of events after the elections. The opportunity must not be lost. Du Plessis, like his colleagues, including De Klerk, was thinking in terms of power-sharing and certainly not of a transfer of power. As he talked of trying to make progress with Buthelezi, I asked the Prime Minister to make clear to him the imperative need to release Mandela, which she proceeded to do.

2 May 1989

I was asked to extract from the South African government, that same day, a response to accusations, made during the trial in Paris of a US arms dealer and three other accused, that South African agents had supplied a rocket launcher and training to a Northern Ireland Protestant paramilitary splinter group. This produced an untypically contrite letter from PW Botha denying that the South Africans had supplied a rocket launcher (it had come from a middleman), but acknowledging that two members of the group had received training in the use of a rocket launcher in South Africa in 1988. Margaret Thatcher replied that the South African ambassador was being asked to send home three members of his staff. The South African arms procurement agency, Armscor, must be told to cease their activities in the United Kingdom.

3 May 1989

FW de Klerk told me that the election would be held on 3 September. He hoped to see the Prime Minister in June. I said that we were concerned about the activities of the lunatic fringes of the security establishment, as evidenced in the missile story from Paris. South Africa could not afford to keep shooting itself in the foot in this way. I warned about military intelligence units 'taking out' enemies of the regime, and that, despite his own orders to terminate support for Renamo, senior officers in military intelligence were continuing arms supplies to them. De Klerk said that any South African president had to retain the support of the armed forces and the police. But he was determined to assert civilian control over the military. I said that we welcomed his statement that after the elections there would have to be negotiations on a new constitution.

In a joint meeting with De Klerk at this time, Harry Oppenheimer and Jan Steyn told me that they too had warned him of the difficulty of knowing exactly what shadowy and criminal elements of the security forces were doing in defiance of any authority from the President.

10 May 1989

In a further discussion with him, De Klerk told me that he envisaged a new constitutional body that would be above the existing houses of parliament. The homelands would become part of a federation.

I observed that Buthelezi had made clear that he would not participate unless Mandela were released. What kind of offer would be made
to the extra-parliamentary opposition?

De Klerk had not worked out an answer to this question. He
was preoccupied with the need to defeat Andries Treurnicht and the
Conservative Party in the elections, in which he would be facing a
strong right-wing challenge in his own constituency of Vereeniging.

18 May 1989

Helen Suzman had a good relationship with FW de Klerk, whom she
had always found to be meticulous and courteous in his dealings with
her, despite their political differences. She told him in parliament that
his statement of intent must be translated into reality. She saw him
not as a starry-eyed liberal, but as a pragmatic, intelligent man who
understood what needed to be done to secure the country's future. He
had not previously had the authority to be able to do so. She quoted
the African saying about not arguing with the crocodile when you
are still in the water – an unmistakable reference to PW Botha. But
now, she said, De Klerk was no longer in the water and could do what
needed to be done to restore peace at home and South Africa's reputation abroad. Above all, he must use his powers to prevent all further
offensive actions by the state.

6 June 1989

I called on PW Botha, who was looking tired and fragile, and was
now very isolated. He asked if we thought the Cubans really would
withdraw from Angola. I said that their withdrawal so far was ahead

of schedule. He made a half-hearted attempt to complain about the Americans, but did not have the energy to finish it. He said that he would be handing over his seals of office in September.

I doubted that he would agree to go gracefully, but felt a sense of great relief and satisfaction at seeing the last of him. For this was a man who never should have been put in charge of the fortunes of his or any other country. For he it was who had personally authorised one of his physicians, Dr Wouter Basson, to develop chemical and biological weapons for use against enemies of the regime.

June 1989

The next step was to arrange for De Klerk to visit Mrs Thatcher at Chequers. This was still an unpopular thing to do; we were accused of colluding with the apartheid regime and the meeting was picketed by the Anti-Apartheid Movement. In fact, Mrs Thatcher made clear to De Klerk, with her customary lack of ambiguity, the need to get on with the Namibia settlement and to release Mandela. She found De Klerk open-minded and a refreshing contrast to PW Botha, but his replies enigmatic. As we stood on the steps at Chequers watching De Klerk's motorcade depart, she told me that she still was uncertain how far he would be prepared to go. I told her that I believed De Klerk would go further than she imagined.

The National Party programme for the elections, however, was a cautious document. The remaining apartheid laws would be eased, or simply not enforced, rather than abolished. The talk of a new constitution was understandably vague. De Klerk had been similarly cautious in a meeting with Chancellor Kohl in Bonn.

There were still many who doubted whether De Klerk's reform-ist language was anything more than a change of style. His brother, Wimpie, who was playing a leading role in the private discussions with the ANC, told me he feared that his brother was far too con-servative to be a good president. I said that he knew his brother better than I did, but I thought FW de Klerk would prove him wrong.

CHAPTER IX

*'You can tell your Prime Minister
she will not be disappointed'*

In spite of De Klerk's successful meetings with the Prime Minister and Chancellor Kohl at the end of June 1989, President George Bush felt unable to invite him to Washington, for fear of difficulties with Congress. The US official responsible for Africa, Hank Cohen, protested in vain that 'it would be a mistake to deal ourselves out of the game' just when it was becoming more interesting.[16]

5 July 1989

PW Botha invited Nelson Mandela to tea with him in his office in the Tuynhuys. Mandela's warder helped him to knot his tie: he had not had much use for one in prison. Niel Barnard, head of the NIS, knelt down to tie Mandela's shoelaces. PW Botha greeted him courteously. Coetsee and Barnard had advised Mandela to avoid raising contentious issues with the President. So they talked about South African history. The meeting lasted less than half an hour. At the end, Mandela asked Botha to release all political prisoners. Botha said that he could not do that.[17]

Mandela was generous about this meeting in his memoirs. What it really amounted to was an attempt by PW Botha to upstage De Klerk and to show that, politically, he was not dead yet. As I pointed out at the time, however, the meeting was going to make it impossible in future to criticise contacts with the ANC.

12 July 1989

In London, Archbishop Trevor Huddleston asked if the Prime Minister would meet Albertina Sisulu, a request strongly supported by me. She had suffered more than most at the hands of the regime, having been detained and banned herself, as well as having had her husband imprisoned for the past twenty-six years. She was held in considerably higher esteem in Soweto than Winnie Mandela, and we had helped to get her son, Zwelakhe, released from detention.

The Prime Minister met her in Downing Street on 12 July. The UDF activist Azhar Cachalia, who was accompanying Albertina, felt that Thatcher lectured, while President Bush, whom they had met in Washington, listened. Albertina was struck by Thatcher's confidence that, after the elections, her husband and Mandela would be released. (Great admirer as I am of George Bush senior, he did not make anything like as strenuous an effort as Thatcher did to bombard the South African government with demands for reform and the release of Mandela. At this time, he and Secretary of State James Baker were preoccupied with the looming collapse of the Soviet Union and, later, the reunification of Germany. South Africa did not figure in George

Bush's principal memoir of his time in the White House and barely registers in those of Baker.[18])

August 1989

It did not take much longer for matters to come to a head with PW Botha. He reacted furiously to an announcement that De Klerk would be meeting President Kaunda in Lusaka, about which he claimed publicly that he had not been consulted, though he had in fact been informed. De Klerk and the cabinet had had enough. In a meeting with President Botha on 14 August, they asked him to retire gracefully, which he declined to do, berating his colleagues instead, displaying in De Klerk's words his 'irascible and cantankerous nature'.[19] They thereupon insisted unanimously on his immediate resignation. The Prime Minister congratulated De Klerk on taking over as President.

September 1989

In the elections, the National Party won ninety-three of the seats, giving them a clear majority in parliament, but lost ground to the Conservative Party, which won thirty-nine seats and around 40 per cent of the Afrikaner votes. The Democratic Party, successor to the Progressive Federal Party, won thirty-three seats.

The election had otherwise been peaceful, but on election day, 6 September, a number of coloured youths were killed in clashes with the police in the Cape townships. Two days later, Archbishop Tutu called for a protest march in Cape Town, on 13 September. Tutu asked me to meet him at Bishopscourt, where he gave me a message for the Prime Minister, urging her to help get the march permitted. Allan

Boesak was also present, sounding as usual more militant than Tutu. From Bishopscourt, I went to see Van Heerden and Pik Botha, who needed no convincing that the march should be authorised; if it were banned, De Klerk's presidency would get off to the worst possible start. But the security chiefs, as usual, were opposed.

Next morning, as I continued my lobbying of the South African government, Johan Heyns walked into my office, accompanied by several other leaders of the Dutch Reformed Church. They had flown down from Pretoria and had heard that we were trying to get the demonstration permitted.

They went off to see De Klerk, determined that he should not start his presidency on the same footing as PW Botha. Overruling the police chiefs, De Klerk agreed to authorise the demonstration. I was asked to help get assurances from the church leaders that, if the police stayed on the sidelines, they would help to guarantee that the demonstration was peaceful. When it took place, we held our breath as a huge crowd assembled. The church and UDF leaders managed effectively to marshal the demonstration, which passed off peacefully.[20]

The Peace March, as it was called, was one of the largest public demonstrations ever in the Cape. It was a turning point in South Africa's history, as De Klerk proceeded to authorise demonstrations in the other major cities. In his first decision as President, he had banned use by the police of the *sjambok* – the hide whips the South African police had employed for decades as one of their favourite methods of crowd control.

In response to Desmond Tutu's message about the planned demonstration in Cape Town, the Prime Minister replied that she was glad the march had been authorised and it had passed off peacefully. She added that she condemned violence from any quarter, including by the police. We had made clear our opposition to detention without trial and had sought to secure the release of the detainees and long-term security prisoners. We wanted the unbanning of the ANC and the lifting of the state of emergency. We were urging De Klerk to make a reality of his promise of dialogue and were working for progress on all the issues of concern to the Archbishop.

The Prime Minister sent a message to congratulate De Klerk. She had high hopes for a new determination to solve South Africa's problems by dialogue. He had described the election result as a clear mandate for reform. He knew the importance she placed on the release of Mandela and Walter Sisulu. He had expressed his intention to draw genuine black leaders into negotiations on a new constitution. She did not underestimate the difficulties, but the first weeks of his administration would be of particular importance. She welcomed the decision to permit the demonstration in Cape Town.

From London, Anthony Sampson asked me and 10 Downing Street for help in ensuring security for ANC president Oliver Tambo's stay in a nursing home in Surrey during his recovery from a stroke. He was assured that appropriate arrangements were being made for Tambo.

20 September 1989

At De Klerk's inauguration as President, as I and the other guests waited in the courtyard of the Union Buildings for the new President to make his speech, Kobie Coetsee rushed up to me. 'Is he going to announce the release of Mandela?' he asked. I said that I did not think so, as that would require preparation, and De Klerk anyway was not the man to take great initiatives without consulting his cabinet.

De Klerk's speech promising negotiations on a new constitution was highly reformist in tone, but non-specific. Patti Waldmeir of the *Financial Times* recorded it in her diary as 'blah, blah, blah'.[21]

21 September 1989

I called on De Klerk in his office in the Union Buildings the following day. He had received the Prime Minister's message. He hoped that we understood that it had not been possible for him to announce specific decisions at his inauguration, with half of his ministers not yet sworn in. He added that his talk with the Prime Minister at Chequers in June had been much tougher than those with other European leaders or with the African presidents. This was because she talked bluntly but frankly and he appreciated that.

I said that we realised that change was going to take time. But the Prime Minister hoped that he would take some practical steps in the near future that would enable us to show, as his decision over the demonstrations in Cape Town, Johannesburg and other centres had done, that real change was going to take place, not just declarations of intent. De Klerk asked about the dates for the upcoming Commonwealth conference, to be held in Kuala Lumpur, which I gave him, while making clear that it was our view that such steps needed to be taken anyway.

I was glad to find that, rather than being alarmed at the advance of the Conservative Party, De Klerk was reaching the opposite conclusion, namely, that 70 per cent of the white population had voted for reform.

The Prime Minister agreed to my suggestion that she should give an interview to Aggrey Klaaste, the outstanding editor of the *Sowetan* (one of South Africa's largest-circulation newspapers), Khulu Sibiya of *City Press* and two other black South African journalists to explain what Britain was trying to achieve in South Africa, namely, the release of Mandela and agreement on a new constitution. She also agreed to see Enos Mabuza again, knowing perfectly well that he was in close touch with the ANC.

The Prime Minister saw Mabuza in Downing Street together with Helen Suzman and Van Zyl Slabbert. All three urged her to seek some positive steps from the South African government before the Commonwealth conference. Helen Suzman did not believe that De Klerk would agree simply to hand over power. But, for the first time, he had aligned the National Party on the liberal side of South African politics. Mabuza said that Thabo Mbeki was ready for negotiations.

October 1989

I pressed Neil van Heerden for a response to the Prime Minister's message, at the time of De Klerk's inauguration, about the need to release the main ANC leaders and draw them into negotiations. I said that I knew all about the resistance, firstly, to doing almost anything, and secondly, to being seen to do anything under foreign pressure, but there was a need to demonstrate that all this *glasnost* (openness) was not just words. Van Heerden said that in permitting the demonstrations in Cape Town and elsewhere, De Klerk had overruled the security establishment. South Africa was pressing ahead with the Namibia agreement. There was no prospect of the early release of Mandela, but we discussed the possible release of the other long-term prisoners, though this would be opposed by General Malan and the police. He added that the Namibia agreement would never have been achieved without our efforts and those of Chester Crocker.

Van Heerden promised that Pik Botha would argue forcefully in the SSC for the release of Walter Sisulu and the other long-term Robben Islanders, but the security establishment would continue to resist. As it was well known that we were pressing for the release of long-term prisoners, the right-wing press were arguing against supposedly giving way to a foreign government on an issue of this kind. I said that, if the South African government wanted to get negotiations under way, the prisoners were going to have to be released. De Klerk had spoken to me of not being able to release Mandela until a climate had been created into which he could be released. This would be a vital step in that direction.

On the evening of 10 October, De Klerk telephoned the Prime Minister to tell her that he was about to announce the release of Walter Sisulu, Ahmed Kathrada, Andrew Mlangeni and five other companions of Mandela on Robben Island. Mandela had been told about this, and that his own release was not at present on the agenda. The Prime Minister was pleased at the news, though she naturally hoped that it would be followed in due course by the release of Mandela.

We were now on the eve of the Commonwealth conference in Kuala Lumpur. I had used its proximity, unashamedly, to accelerate the release of Walter Sisulu and his companions. Given these positive moves by De Klerk, Margaret Thatcher was determined to support him and more than ever disposed to resist further sanctions. In this, she was fully justified; if the release of the senior ANC leaders had been followed by more punitive actions, this would have played into the hands of De Klerk's conservative opponents within the Afrikaner community.

She enjoyed the ensuing fracas with most of the other Commonwealth heads of government, determined to ignore what actually was happening in South Africa, rather more than her new Foreign Secretary, John Major. The Australian prime minister, Bob Hawke, Kenneth Kaunda and others all argued for more sanctions. The assembled foreign ministers came up with a communiqué John Major and the Foreign Office officials felt they could 'live with'. Considering that it paid no regard whatever to the positive developments in South Africa, Margaret Thatcher proceeded to issue a statement of her own, paying tribute to those changes and suggesting that the Commonwealth should concentrate on encouraging them, rather than on further punishment.

Hawke and the Canadian prime minister, Brian Mulroney, protested at this appalling breach of etiquette. She got a terrible press in Britain, suggesting that she had disavowed John Major, though he had in fact approved her statement, and noting that she was once more 'isolated'. Given that within four months De Klerk was to announce the release of Mandela, her stand and the statement she issued made a great deal more sense than theirs did.

26 October 1989

I went to Soweto to meet Walter Sisulu and the other released Robben Islanders. They were grateful for the international support that had been shown for them. I told them that I had spoken to the government about the need not to interfere with the planned rally to welcome them back to Soweto. We would be intensifying our efforts to get Mandela released in the new year. This would depend on the demonstrations remaining peaceful. Walter Sisulu said that he would be seeking to ensure this.

It was an emotional occasion to meet at last these legendary figures in the history of the ANC. None of these venerable gentlemen, wearing cardigans or waistcoats, looked very much like revolutionaries, though several were members of the SACP. I was pleased, especially, for Albertina Sisulu, who had conducted herself with as much dignity as they had, and who told me that she was finding it quite strange to have her husband, Walter, back home again!

In his public statements following his release, Sisulu continued to emphasise the armed struggle. He also called for more sanctions, though with no expectation that they would actually be imposed.

As De Klerk was continuing to talk about the need to protect group rights, I suggested to Gerrit Viljoen and others that this terminology should be changed to emphasise minority rights. De Klerk told me that he was not in the business of 'reforming himself out of power'. What he was thinking of at this time was power-sharing, not a transfer of power. I told the Prime Minister that De Klerk was a calm and rational man, who was not going to fall back into the arms of the security establishment. He was trying to create conditions in which it should be possible to release Mandela.

November 1989

In June, Lech Walesa and Solidarity had achieved victory in legislative elections in Poland, paving the way for the end of Communist rule and a transition to full democracy in that country. In October, the dismissal of Erich Honecker had signalled the imminent collapse of Communist rule in East Germany. Following the opening of the borders, the destruction of the Berlin Wall began on 10 November.

De Klerk by now had reached the conclusion that he would not be able to get meaningful constitutional negotiations under way without releasing Mandela, and that Mandela might well prove to be a moderating influence in those negotiations. Discussing with him the developments in Eastern Europe, I found that he had grasped the full significance of the impending collapse of the Soviet Union, discrediting the securocrat doctrine of the 'total onslaught' and weakening Soviet support for the ANC.

December 1989

I discussed the issue of Mandela's release again with Van Heerden. Gerrit Viljoen, the Minister for Constitutional Development, and Pik Botha wanted this to happen early in the new year, though some members of the government wanted an agreement on negotiations to be worked out first.

Mandela, meanwhile, had conveyed to De Klerk his appreciation for the release of his comrades. He had observed the authorisation of demonstrations that would have been banned under PW Botha, the scrapping by De Klerk of the militaristic NSMS, the opening up of beaches hitherto reserved for whites and the planned abolition of the

Separate Amenities Act, concluding that there was indeed a new hand on the tiller. He wrote a letter to De Klerk, as he had to PW Botha, urging talks between the government and the ANC, but reiterating that the ANC would not accept any preconditions, especially not suspension of the armed struggle.

13 December 1989

Mandela met De Klerk at the Tuynhuys. De Klerk, who was accompanied by Kobie Coetsee and Niel Barnard, head of the NIS, 'listened to what I had to say. This was a novel experience.' Mandela said that the National Party concept of 'group rights' was seen by his people as a way to preserve a form of apartheid. According to Mandela, De Klerk's response was: 'We will have to change it, then.'[22]

Mandela said that, if the government did not unban the ANC, when released he would be working for a banned organisation and would be liable to be rearrested. Mandela's report to his colleagues in Lusaka, in a deliberate echo of Margaret Thatcher's comment about Gorbachev, was that De Klerk was a man they could do business with.

I saw Pik Botha shortly after De Klerk's meeting with Mandela, which De Klerk told him had gone well. Pik Botha expected Mandela's release to be decided within weeks.

9 January 1990

I returned to London to discuss with the new Foreign Secretary, Douglas Hurd – John Major having moved to become Chancellor of the Exchequer – and the Prime Minister what our response should be to the release of Mandela. The Prime Minister wanted a strongly positive response by us, agreeing with my suggestion that we should lift the voluntary ban on new investment if De Klerk took steps also to open the way for negotiations. De Klerk was invited to visit her again at Chequers, provided there was progress in that direction. She agreed that we must redouble our efforts now to get South Africa to sign the Nuclear Non-Proliferation Treaty. A visit by her to South Africa would have to wait until later, but Douglas Hurd should visit South Africa at the time of the Namibian independence celebrations, scheduled for 21 March.

10 January 1990

I heard that De Klerk had made a remarkable speech, in private, to the hierarchy of the South African Police. In it he said that, for too long, the police had been asked to solve South Africa's political problems. Henceforth this must be the task of the political leaders. For the resulting unrest had been like a bush fire. If stamped out in one place on the veld, it simply flared up in another. More fighting would not lead to victory, but to racial conflagration: 'For if this Armageddon takes place – and blood flows ankle deep in our streets and four or five million people lie dead – the problem will remain exactly the same as it was before the shooting started.'

23 January 1990

I had an hour's talk with De Klerk on his own. I gave him the Prime Minister's congratulations on the progress he was making and told him about Douglas Hurd's plan to visit South Africa, which he welcomed. He accepted the Prime Minister's invitation to meet him again in May. Their last meeting had been valuable to him. He expected to have made a good deal of progress by then.

De Klerk said that he was in intense discussions with the senior members of his cabinet. They were addressing all the obstacles to getting negotiations under way – Mandela, the state of emergency, whether the ANC could be unbanned and the ANC's attitude to violence. He could not yet tell us what he would say in his speech to parliament on 2 February, but would give the Prime Minister an indication in advance. This would not, he assured me, be another 'Rubicon' speech, which had so disappointed everybody. He was determined to make progress.

I argued that unbanning the ANC was the only way to propel them into negotiations. If the release of Mandela were not addressed in his speech in terms of intent, there would be great disappointment. De Klerk said that it would be addressed. But Mandela's release had to be managed in a way that would help to trigger negotiations.

De Klerk said that it was important that there should be a positive Western response. He had raised this with the US Assistant Secretary of State for African Affairs, Hank Cohen, without getting any very positive reaction. I said that, if he made progress on these issues, there would be a positive response from us.

We discussed the ANC statement expressing support for negotiations, but also the supposed need to intensify the armed struggle. I said that there had been no recent ANC attacks on civilian targets. We would go on arguing for a suspension of violence.

I raised also the issue of abolition of the death penalty. We welcomed the sharp increase in the number of cases in which death sentences had been commuted. It would make a positive impact if a review could be announced. De Klerk clearly intended to do something about this.

1 February 1990

At midnight, De Klerk telephoned me at the embassy in Cape Town to say: 'You can tell your Prime Minister that she will not be disappointed.' He added that the US media were reporting that he would announce Mandela's immediate release. He had discussed this with Mandela, who was himself insisting that time should be taken to make proper arrangements. His speech to parliament would contain an announcement of the intention to release Mandela. There would be other dramatic announcements.

I thanked him for forewarning us and told 10 Downing Street that the ANC and all other banned organisations would be unbanned, Mandela's release would follow shortly, the death penalty would be reviewed and there would be a justiciable declaration of rights in the new constitution.

CHAPTER X

'After today, South Africa will never be the same'

2 February 1990

We gathered next morning, in our morning suits, the women all in hats, for the opening of parliament. There was a sense of excitement in the chamber as De Klerk stood up to speak. From the outset he signalled that this was going to be no ordinary speech, declaring with heavy emphasis that the 'season of violence' was over: the time for reconciliation had arrived. Andries Treurnicht and his Conservative Party cohorts walked out as De Klerk announced the unbanning of the ANC and the South African Communist Party, the freeing of political prisoners, the suspension of capital punishment and the lifting of many of the restrictions imposed under the state of emergency. Then came the announcement the world had been waiting for: 'I wish to put it plainly that the Government has taken a firm decision to release Mr Mandela unconditionally.'

On his way to parliament, De Klerk had said to his wife: 'After today, South Africa will never be the same.' For De Klerk was proclaiming nothing less than a constitutional revolution. One of my friends in the ANC, Cheryl Carolus, at that moment was making a fiery speech to a huge crowd in Greenmarket Square, urging them to march on parliament, an idea that had to be abandoned when she heard, to her amazement, what De Klerk had done.

The Prime Minister sent a message to De Klerk applauding his decision to release Mandela unconditionally, thereby unblocking the way for negotiations on a new constitution. She welcomed the unbanning of the ANC. The British government would henceforth be encouraging a policy of contacts with South Africa and would consider what further steps we could take once Mandela was free.

I passed this to De Klerk, who replied that there were no longer any reasonable grounds for South Africa to be isolated. 'I assure you that Mr Nelson Mandela will shortly be a free man.' He looked forward to meeting her at Chequers in May.

I told Van Heerden that we would lift the ban on new investment as soon as Mandela was released on a basis that would trigger negotiations on a new constitution. De Klerk had promised to review all the remaining emergency restrictions if the ANC agreed to negotiations. We recognised that De Klerk and his colleagues were taking considerable political risks and deserved support. Douglas Hurd set about the uphill struggle of seeking to persuade other European Community governments of this, as did the Prime Minister with her European counterparts and President Bush.

Pik Botha made an impassioned plea to the European ambassadors for a more positive response from their governments. It was absurd to describe the fundamental changes De Klerk was making as merely 'a step in the right direction'. To do so helped only Treurnicht and the right-wing backlash. The British response had helped, as it included something tangible (the encouragement of scientific, cultural, academic and other contacts).

In a separate discussion with me, Pik Botha said that all the remaining apartheid laws would be repealed. Virtually all the troops had been withdrawn from the townships. The government was ready to discuss an amnesty with the ANC.

10 February 1990

The Prime Minister and I were informed that De Klerk would announce Mandela's release that afternoon. The Prime Minister announced that Britain would lift the ban on new investment and urged other countries to do the same.

11 February 1990

Mandela was released from Victor Verster prison, near Paarl, and met with a tumultuous and chaotic reception in Cape Town. The crowd was so dense that his car initially was unable to get through to the City Hall, where he was to address the throng assembled on the Grand Parade. On this great day, I was delighted to have staying with us in the embassy Anthony and Sally Sampson. Anthony Sampson, who had known Mandela well before he was imprisoned and was a great friend of Oliver Tambo, had helped me in my own contacts with the ANC.

Mandela's speech, written for him by the UDF on instructions from the ANC in Lusaka, fell a long way short of matching this historic occasion. Amid a welter of hardline rhetoric, he reaffirmed his commitment to the armed struggle, though he added the hope that a climate conducive to a negotiated settlement would be created soon so that there might no longer be a need for armed struggle. 'I am a loyal and disciplined member of the African National Congress,' in full agreement with its policies and strategies, including that of nationalisation, he declared. He had not entered into negotiations with the government. 'Now is the time to intensify the struggle on all fronts.' He accepted that 'Mr De Klerk himself is a man of integrity'. But he called on the international community to maintain sanctions and continue to isolate the regime. The *Financial Times* correspondent, Patti Waldmeir, described it as 'a speech from hell'.[23]

12 February 1990

On the following day, the real voice of Mandela was heard during a press conference in the gardens of Archbishop Tutu's house in Bishopscourt. He said that the ANC were concerned to address white fears over the principle of one person, one vote. They were ready to discuss guarantees to ensure that this did not result in black domination of whites. 'The whites are our fellow South Africans. We want them to feel safe.' He recognised their contribution to the development of the country. He had sought not to negotiate, but to act as a facilitator between the ANC and the government. He repeated that De Klerk was a man of integrity, but there was no reason to lift sanctions. He did not want confrontation, but negotiations. The ANC were correct to pursue a policy of nationalisation.

Apart from one very agitated call to me by Pik Botha, the

government so far were reacting calmly to Mandela's call for continuance of the armed struggle.

16 February 1990

Two-hour meeting with Mandela in Johannesburg with some of my ambassadorial colleagues. I was greeted with great friendliness by Mandela, who said that he would like a more private discussion and, to the surprise of the attendant television crews, asked for his best wishes to be passed to the Prime Minister.

Mandela expressed appreciation for the international support he had received, without which he could have been forgotten. For three years he had been discussing with the government how to bring them into a discussion with the ANC. He wanted a peaceful settlement. The state of emergency must be lifted and all politically motivated prisoners released, on the basis of an amnesty. He had been impressed by his discussion with De Klerk. South Africa was fortunate to have him as its head of state. De Klerk did want to write a new chapter in South Africa's history, as did Coetsee and Viljoen. But apartheid still existed. He had told De Klerk that no solution could be found on the basis of group rights; sanctions and the armed struggle must continue. He concluded by asking for help from us. In his view, Mrs Thatcher had played a crucial role in bringing the US and the Soviet Union together. She had led the way in persuading Mikhail Gorbachev and Ronald Reagan that they could do business together. These were breathtaking developments.

I said that we were discussing with the government the removal of the remaining obstacles to a negotiation. We believed that they would soon lift the state of emergency. I had discussed on a number of occasions with De Klerk and Viljoen the question of group rights, and had urged them to think rather along the lines of the protection of minority rights, the term Mandela himself was using. An amnesty for political prisoners was likely to be agreed in the process of negotiations. We hoped that, once negotiations were engaged, the armed struggle would be suspended.

In a brief discussion with Mandela afterwards, since he had referred to the Boer leader General Christiaan de Wet in arguing for the release of prisoners, I told him that I had many times used the same example in arguing for his own release. Mandela asked me for help with Pik Botha about organising his passport, which Pik Botha assured me would be delivered immediately.

20 February 1990

Meeting in Soweto with Walter Sisulu, who had been appointed chairman of the internal wing of the ANC, and his deputy, Ahmed Kathrada. I explained that, when De Klerk had visited Britain the year before, we had urged him to take all the steps he had now taken and we had told him that, if he did so, there would be a response, at any rate from Britain. We had therefore reversed the discouragement of contacts with South Africa and of new investment, but the arms, oil and nuclear embargoes remained in place. I added that we did exert pressure for change, but in a way different from other governments. Mandela had telephoned me to ask if I could help to persuade De Klerk to release Peter Mokaba, head of the South African Youth Council (later superseded by the reconstituted ANC Youth League), from detention. Their own release, and that of Mandela, had owed a great deal to the pressure by the Prime Minister.

Both said that they were well aware of this, and so was Mandela. Ahmed Kathrada said that he had stated publicly that the Prime Minister's efforts had contributed to these developments and that, while he differed with us over sanctions, he would not criticise the British government himself for that reason.

I said that, if De Klerk did not get some encouragement for the steps he had taken, it would be harder for him to go further. We were not going to treat him as if he were PW Botha. Walter Sisulu said that we had been more directly involved than others in obtaining these results, but he was worried that we might start leading a general crusade against sanctions. I said that we would not, but at some point I would be asking the ANC to consider suspending the sports boycott.

I made a first attempt to ask them to reconsider the ANC position on nationalisation. If the banks and mines were nationalised without compensation, there would be no further investment in the country. If compensation were paid, there would be no funding available for anything else.

These two highly impressive ANC leaders accepted the need to reflect on this issue. It would, they said, have to be discussed exhaustively within the ANC. I thanked Walter Sisulu for planning to visit Natal to see if he could help to reduce the violence between the ANC and Inkatha. I argued for an early meeting between Mandela and Buthelezi.

Our contacts with the ANC at this time were a good deal closer than was generally realised. On a couple of occasions while I was on leave, Anthony Sampson had arranged private meetings for me with Oliver Tambo at his house in Highgate, where Tambo's wife, Adelaide, had plied me with currant cake. I was very impressed by the scholarly and thoughtful Tambo, who clearly was committed to a negotiated solution to his country's problems. An unlikely revolutionary, when Mandela was released he invited me to dinner in London with him with a card bearing the words 'Carriages at eleven o'clock!' My colleagues in Lusaka had long since established close relationships with Thabo Mbeki and Jacob Zuma.

22 February 1990

Walter Sisulu rang to say that Mandela wanted to see me in Soweto. I met him in the tiny matchbox-style house he had returned to, not wanting at first to move into his wife's much larger house in Diepkloof, nicknamed by the Sowetans 'Beverly Hills'. The contrast was dramatic between these humble surroundings and the quality of the man inside. Mandela in this period had not yet adopted the batik shirts he later made so famous, instead appearing in immaculate Prince of Wales tweed suits made for him by his friend and tailor, Yusuf Surtee.

His old-world courtesy and unfailing charm served to mask a steely determination not to compromise any of the principles for which he and others had sacrificed their liberty or lives. He was, he kept emphasising, the servant of his party, the African National Congress, and not its master. It was, he insisted to me, not a party, but a movement intended to embody the aspirations of all South Africans. He had difficulty accepting that the ANC could be wrong, and even in understanding that others might not want to join it. Yet he showed a much greater commitment than others to genuine political tolerance and acceptance that South Africa must be a society with which all sections of the population could identify, including his former oppressors.

I explained to Mandela the efforts the Prime Minister personally had made with De Klerk, Pik Botha and their colleagues to help secure his release and a commitment to negotiations. Having urged them to take this major step, we had to respond, and were doing so by rescinding the voluntary embargoes on tourism and new investment. The other embargoes would continue, but it made no sense to discourage academic and scientific contacts with the liberal English-speaking universities, where we were supporting a number of black students.

Mandela said that he understood the role the Prime Minister had played and the efforts I had made to help secure his release and that of Walter Sisulu and others, as well as the unbanning of the ANC. But the process of political change had only just begun and international pressure must be maintained. I said that we agreed with this, but we were doing so in a way different from other countries, through much more direct engagement with the South African government. Mandela himself had stressed the importance of De Klerk's being able to take the National Party with him, and there were obvious difficulties with the security forces. We would be pressing the government to lift the state of emergency. Over political prisoners, I had talked to Gerrit Viljoen, the Minister for Constitutional Development, and there would be progress towards an amnesty.

I said that we could not agree with other ANC demands. Ideas that an interim government should be established, or elections to a constituent assembly held, before any agreement on the future constitution had been reached were non-starters; they amounted to a demand that majority rule should be established before negotiations had taken place.

Mandela indicated that he believed that only two conditions – lifting the state of emergency and an amnesty for political prisoners – needed to be met before negotiations could be engaged. I asked if, on that basis, the ANC would commit themselves formally to a suspension of violence, and Mandela said that he thought they should. I raised the issue of the violence in Natal. Mandela said that he had been able to maintain good personal relations with Buthelezi and he hoped that these could be used to stop the killings.

Mandela added that he had a high personal regard for the Prime Minister and wanted to 'get her on my side'. But he hoped that Margaret Thatcher would not visit South Africa until matters were much further advanced. He was under instructions from the ANC in Lusaka not to meet the Foreign Secretary, Douglas Hurd, during his visit to South Africa en route to Namibia; the ANC remained opposed to ministerial visits at this time.

I pointed out that the ANC's position was illogical. Mandela himself had been urging us to use our influence with the South African government to promote further change. How could we be expected to do that without seeing them at a senior level? Mandela talked about meeting Douglas Hurd in Namibia, but the ANC would agree only if there were no prior visit by him to South Africa.

Mandela said that he would be visiting London to attend the concert at Wembley Stadium celebrating his release, on 16 April. He wanted to meet the Prime Minister, but would have to get the agreement of the ANC. He had said publicly that he wanted to talk to her about sanctions. I said that it would be a mistake not to meet the Prime Minister in London and Mandela clearly thought so too.

As the oil giant Mobil recently had disinvested, leaving us being asked to bail out projects they had been supporting in Soweto, I asked Mandela not to call for further disinvestment, explaining why. Mandela said that he could not change the ANC line on disinvestment. I said that he did not need to; all I was asking was that he should not call for it himself (and, as a matter of fact, he never did).

The Prime Minister, not surprisingly, found Mandela's deference to his ANC colleagues disappointing. Mandela told me subsequently that he was annoyed with them for opposing a meeting with her during the Wembley visit and had made clear that he would be doing so on the next occasion (the US embassy were told that he was 'furious' with Zwelakhe Sisulu for leading the opposition to such a meeting[24]).

Meanwhile, he needed some practical help from us. Not wanting to rely for his security only on the South African police, he asked us to provide training for his personal bodyguards, which we arranged for the SAS to do. Later on, when he moved to his wife's much larger house, he asked for our help in providing better privacy and security there.

25 February 1990
The violence continued in Natal. I had urged Mandela to hold a meeting as soon as possible with Chief Buthelezi, reminding him that Buthelezi had refused to negotiate with the government until he was

released. Mandela told me that he had telephoned Buthelezi after his release and wanted to meet him. But, as he records in *Long Walk to Freedom*, when he visited the ANC leadership in Lusaka, the idea of such a meeting was rejected.[25]

Mandela, addressing a huge crowd in Durban, urged them to 'Take your guns, your knives and your pangas and throw them into the sea! ... End this war now!' But, because of the opposition of the ANC leaders in Natal, led by Harry Gwala, a planned meeting with Buthelezi was cancelled. Mandela told me that, when he mentioned the possibility of a meeting with Buthelezi in Pietermaritzburg, he found the crowd muttering against it. He and Sisulu made a failed attempt instead to meet the Zulu monarch, King Goodwill Zwelithini.

The decision to cancel the joint meeting with Buthelezi was a serious mistake. On his return from exile, I discovered that the leading Zulu in the ANC politburo, Jacob Zuma, strongly agreed with me about this. It was, in his view, a fatal error not to have arranged from the outset a meeting with Buthelezi and a joint call for peace, instead of giving in to the opposition of the ANC in Natal. The better part of a year was to elapse before such a meeting took place, leaving Buthelezi aggrieved and the violence worse than ever. Jacob Zuma later was to make great efforts himself to reduce the clashes with Inkatha.

March 1990

Following police shootings in Sebokeng in which eleven people were killed, Mandela threatened to postpone indefinitely talks with the government. The police action was indefensible and was criticised by De Klerk, but over four hundred people had been killed in unrest since the unbanning of the ANC and much of the mayhem had been caused by the teenage 'comrades'.

Mangosuthu Buthelezi saw the Prime Minister in London. She expressed disappointment at Mandela's refusal to suspend the armed struggle and at the continued references to nationalisation. Buthelezi said that, nevertheless, Mandela was a 'bigger man than the others' and this would eventually show.

I reported that the unbanning of the ANC inevitably had triggered a wave of unrest in the townships. When I saw De Klerk, I found him reacting calmly to this, but he said he could not remove the remaining emergency regulations until there was a period of calm.

Walter Sisulu told me that the ANC were in no hurry to start negotiations. They wanted the release of all political prisoners, including those convicted of violent crimes. The government were acknowledging privately the case for a general amnesty in due course, particularly given the equally violent record of members of the security forces.

Peter Mokaba, on his release from detention, proceeded to distinguish himself by making inflammatory speeches about 'one Boer, one bullet'. I telephoned Mandela to say that, having asked me to help get him released, now he needed to tell Mokaba to shut up. Mandela, with disingenuous charm, declared that 'the young man must have been misquoted', but we heard no more from Mokaba, a highly dubious individual, about one Boer, one bullet.

19 March 1990

When Douglas Hurd and I saw De Klerk, he did not rule out an amnesty. He was concerned at what he regarded as delaying tactics by the ANC. The talks with the government, when they were engaged, would focus on the release of prisoners and return of exiles. De Klerk was determined not to be thrown off track by temporary setbacks.

In the future constitution, he considered the key to be the protection of minority rights. He had no blueprint for this, but there had to be recognition of the pluralism of South African society. He wanted to move away from the definition of groups, which was unacceptable, and favoured a bill of rights. But the protection of individual rights would not of itself protect minorities. He talked of some form of power-sharing, and was, he said, in a hurry in his search for a solution. The ship he had launched would never be turned around, but he was not about to commit suicide. Mandela's continuing references to nationalisation reflected the long-standing policy of the ANC. Douglas Hurd observed that all Mandela's pronouncements currently were accorded a mystical reverence, whether they made sense or not.

De Klerk and Pik Botha told Douglas Hurd that, for South Africa to sign the Nuclear Non-Proliferation Treaty, they needed our help in getting the neighbouring countries to do so as well, even though, obviously, the effect would be purely symbolic. Hurd concluded that De Klerk, bent on dismantling apartheid and the South African military nuclear programme, was 'an amazingly brave and wise man'.

20 March 1990

Gerrit Viljoen said that the upsurge in violence was partly attributable to continued ANC emphasis on the armed struggle. Mandela understood the need to meet white concerns in the new constitution, but these would not be allayed if simple majority voting in a unitary state

126

were accepted from the outset. Otherwise, they could be managed. I said that the issue of greatest concern to Mandela was the release of prisoners. Viljoen said there could not be early release for those convicted of 'gross' crimes. There would need to be an amnesty in stages.

There followed a meeting at the embassy with the two recently released Delmas treason trialists, Popo Molefe (secretary-general of the UDF) and Mosiuoa 'Terror' Lekota. The meeting was opposed by some of their colleagues, but they had not forgotten the support we had showed for them by visiting the courtroom when they were on trial for their lives. They were trying to calm things down in the townships. They did not distrust De Klerk's motives, but had no reason to trust the security forces. They wanted us to maintain sanctions. But they knew that we had argued hard for their release and wanted us to continue to use our influence with the South African government.

On a visit we arranged to some of the projects we were supporting in the Cape townships, Douglas Hurd was surprised to find himself being escorted around Crossroads by an honour guard of young black South Africans carrying wooden rifles and chanting 'Viva Tambo!', but took this in his stride.

*　*　*

On the following day, Douglas Hurd and I flew in to Windhoek for the Namibia independence celebrations. It was not without some dramas that this goal finally had been reached.

Martti Ahtisaari and Prem Chand had continued to experience difficulties with the South African government, requiring frequent interventions by us, over the return of Swapo leaders and refugees. When the Swapo leaders did return to Windhoek, I invited Hage Geingob (who became prime minister on Namibia's independence), Theo-Ben Gurirab (foreign minister) and Hidipo Hamutenya (later Minister of Trade and Industry) to lunch at the Kalahari Sands Hotel. We had kept in touch with them throughout their years of exile. I explained that I did not expect them to feel any particular affinity with a Conservative government in Britain, or vice versa. We did not agree with their quasi-Marxist economic views and hoped that they would change them. But we were determined to see that they were given a fair chance in free elections and I expected them to win. If they did, we would help the new government to get established. The response was positive. The Swapo leaders made clear that they were determined to preserve the Namibian economy. I encouraged them to visit the Rössing uranium mine, which they did shortly afterwards and were as impressed as I had been by what they found there.

Not long afterwards, the leading white member of Swapo, lawyer Anton Lubowski, was assassinated. I had got to know him quite well and had no doubt that this exploit was the work of the criminals in the CCB. It was a black day when I attended his funeral in the township, where Theo-Ben Gurirab made an emotional appeal for calm.

October 1990

As the Namibian elections, due in November, drew closer I also had no doubt that we would witness a final attempt by South African military intelligence to disrupt them. What could not be predicted was the form this would take.

One day in Pretoria I suddenly was summoned, with the other Western ambassadors, to an urgent meeting with Pik Botha and General Jannie Geldenhuys, the Chief of the SADF. Pik Botha read out intercepted radio messages which purported to show that another massive Swapo incursion was planned, with the connivance of the Kenyan battalion of Untag, the UN force. As British military personnel controlled the UN's communications in Namibia, it took me about three hours to discover, and not much longer to warn Van Heerden, that these messages were false. A furious Pik Botha had been misled by his own intelligence services. As usual, no action appeared to be taken against those responsible for this deception.

21 March 1990

The crisis passed, with Swapo winning the elections by a large margin. Douglas Hurd and I attended the celebrations in Windhoek to mark Namibia's independence. It was a chaotic evening, with Pérez de Cuéllar and various heads of state barely able to get into the stadium and PLO leader Yasser Arafat attempting to accost James Baker, who was by no means anxious to meet him. But there also was no doubting the sense of joy, and also of relief, among the immense crowd gathered there at the attainment of self-rule and the end of a long and bitter conflict.

CHAPTER XI

---❖---

'You can be Mandela and I'll be Mrs Thatcher'

March 1990

On his return to London, Douglas Hurd reported to the Prime Minister that the government and the ANC were edging their way towards 'talks about talks'. De Klerk had appeared unruffled. The emergency powers would be relaxed as soon as the violence abated. But there were in the townships large groups of radicalised, uneducated teenagers engaged in violence.

Hurd saw Mandela briefly at the independence dinner in Windhoek. Mandela was friendly, apologised for the fact that a meeting had not taken place and offered one for the next day, by which time Hurd had to leave.

On my return to Cape Town, Van Heerden told me that, in his meeting with De Klerk, Mandela had attacked the conduct of the police, not only at Sebokeng, but in the townships generally. But the wave of violence across the country over the past eight weeks had not been triggered by the police, and the ANC needed to discipline their own supporters. De Klerk wanted to lift the emergency restrictions as soon as he could. A lot of prisoners had already been released and more would follow. De Klerk could not consider an immediate amnesty for those responsible for 'necklace' killings and bombings. There would be progress in removing obstacles to the return of the exiles.

12 April 1990

The Soviet foreign minister, Eduard Shevardnadze, commented favourably to Douglas Hurd on his own meeting with De Klerk, also in Windhoek. The Russians, he said, should use their influence with the ANC and we should use ours with the South African government.

For the ANC, the obstacles to negotiations were the state of emergency and the delay in the release of prisoners; for the government, it was the mayhem in the townships. I asked Viljoen's deputy, Roelf Meyer, if the state of emergency could be restricted to Natal. Beyond that, it would have a positive effect to establish a programme for the repeal of the remaining apartheid laws. The government would be wasting its time unless it was prepared to deal directly with the issue of one person, one vote. Meyer said that, personally, he agreed, provided they could entrench an independent judiciary and a justiciable bill of rights. Ways would have to be found to assure the whites and other minorities that their interests could not be overridden by the majority. No one had yet come up with a viable solution to this problem.

16 April 1990

Mandela arrived in London for the Wembley concert to celebrate his release. A crowd of seventy-two thousand packed Wembley Stadium for the star-studded concert, which was broadcast live to more than sixty countries. Mandela received an eight-minute standing ovation when he took the stage.

The Prime Minister, however, reacted with incredulity to a statement by him criticising her planned meeting with De Klerk, whom she had helped to persuade to release him. Nor did she consider that such a meeting required the permission of the ANC. But Mandela also said publicly that he would be returning soon to London to meet her and, as he had told me, that she was 'a very powerful lady – one I would rather have as an ally than an enemy'.[26]

Pik Botha argued that the Population Registration Act, the 1950 law that first elaborated the apartheid system of race classification, would automatically disappear with the passage of a new constitution. I said that it would be far better to repeal it beforehand. We had impressed on the ANC that there must be no further postponement of talks with the government and that they would not succeed in their demand for the setting-up of a constituent assembly prior to deciding the new constitution.

Van Heerden told me that the government had evidence that elements of the ANC did not believe in the negotiating process. I said that the ANC were saying exactly the same to me about elements of the security forces.

19 April 1990

De Klerk made a speech to parliament in which he accepted for the first time the possibility of universal suffrage based on a common voters' roll and set out a timetable for the repeal of the remaining apartheid legislation (the Separate Amenities Act, the Group Areas Act and the Population Registration Act). De Klerk continued to reject the notion of 'black majority rule' on the grounds that no community should be pre-eminent over the others.

The Prime Minister told Gerrit Viljoen, in London, that De Klerk's speech the previous day had been another major step forward. She was disappointed that Mandela continued to defer to his ANC colleagues, rather than leading from the front. Viljoen said he was thinking of possible entrenched representation for the minorities in an upper house.

I reported on the tensions between Thabo Mbeki and MK leader Chris Hani, who felt that the ANC were simply being led into a trap. Desmond Tutu and Kenneth Kaunda both by now were calling for suspension of the armed struggle, and the ANC were having difficulty controlling their own supporters. The overthrow of the intensely unpopular homeland government in Ciskei on 4 March, a coup in which twenty-seven people were killed, had been followed by looting and arson.

As these scenes unfolded, I telephoned Terror Lekota at the ANC headquarters in Johannesburg and asked him and his colleagues to do something about this, given that we were trying to persuade De Klerk to lift the state of emergency. To his credit, Lekota did rush to the Ciskei and some semblance of order was restored.

Barend du Plessis assured me that the government were not going to be pushed off course by the violence. There would be progress with Mandela on the release of prisoners. I said that I hoped the government would stop denouncing 'simplistic majority rule'. They would do better to insist on the need for constitutional guarantees and a genuine multiparty system. Du Plessis replied that what the government were concerned to avoid was 'democracy African style'.

2 May 1990

In the run-up to the first meeting between the South African government and the ANC, held at the historic Groote Schuur ('great barn') residence of Cecil Rhodes in Cape Town, the government tried to resist the inclusion of white South Africa's *bête noire*, Joe Slovo, in the ANC delegation, only for Mandela to insist that he be included. (As described later, Joe Slovo at times was to prove a moderating influence on his colleagues in the ANC.) In personal terms, the two sides got on better than they had expected, each proving to the other that, as Mbeki said, 'they did not have horns'.[27]

In the meeting, Mandela said that he was not sure that De Klerk would be able to carry the National Party and its supporters along with him on the course he had chosen. However, at the conclusion of the talks, De Klerk said that he looked to the future with confidence. Mandela said that the meeting was 'the realisation of a dream', given all the ANC's efforts through its history to engage with the government. The ANC would look into the whole question of the armed struggle. Sanctions should not be lifted, but it should not be necessary to ask for them to be intensified.

Mandela, however, was sticking to the ANC demands for the establishment of an interim government and a constituent assembly. I told him again that we would support him over the emergency laws and release of prisoners, but not over these demands, which had no chance of being accepted.

Pik Botha told us that an indemnity from prosecution had been agreed, which would be applied across the board, and would cover both ANC and security force miscreants. The state of emergency would be re-examined in the context of a commitment to reduce violence. Mandela had effectively said that continued references to the 'armed struggle' were largely rhetoric. They had agreed to a 'common commitment ... to a peaceful process of negotiations'. Crucially, the talks had been held in a cordial atmosphere, and members of the government had got on well with their ANC counterparts.

May 1990

De Klerk made a successful eighteen-day visit to Europe, during which he held talks with the Prime Minister, Chancellor Kohl, French president François Mitterrand and other European leaders. There was still as yet no formal relaxation of sanctions by the European Community, but the member states had lost interest in enforcing them. De Klerk received a warm reception from the Prime Minister at Chequers. In his words, 'Once she had decided that she could trust me, and that I would do what I said I was going to do, she did everything that she could to support me.'[28]

On his return, De Klerk felt that the sanctions tide had turned. I told Van Heerden that this would depend on what the government did about the release of prisoners and the state of emergency.

4 June 1990

Further meeting with Mandela. He had told an astonished crowd of his supporters in Soweto to learn Afrikaans, which he had done while in prison, better to understand the minds of their antagonists and to start disarming them by addressing them in their own language. I recalled, to laughter from Mandela, that the last political leader to require this of the Sowetans had been Dr Treurnicht, whose attempt to introduce Afrikaans in the schools had led to the 1976 Soweto uprising.

On the future constitution, I said that we were committed to one person, one vote, and majority government, but did not regard these as incompatible with the sort of protection for minority rights that existed in other democratic constitutions. Nor did Mandela, he said, though not on the basis of 'group rights'. Ways would have to be found to address this.

I said that, since he was asking us to use our influence with the South African government, in particular to lift the state of emergency, we knew what they would accept and what they would not. The ANC still were placing great emphasis on the demand for the election of a constituent assembly, which had no chance of being agreed and which we did not support ourselves, as that would entail majority rule before the constitution was written. Mandela said that there was strong pressure from within the movement for this, but he understood the point I was making.

Mandela, in a revealing aside, said that, if he had achieved a prominent position, it was because of the organisation. No political leader was of any value unless he could take his constituency with him. If he lost the support of his party, it would remain only for him to write his memoirs. Black South Africans had suffered terrible things for forty years under leaders such as Verwoerd, Vorster and Botha. Three million people had been forcibly removed. Thousands had been killed by the police. Police shootings – though not the fault of De Klerk – were continuing even now. All this had left an enormous residue of bitterness and militancy. He would want to explain this to the Prime Minister, but also to assure her of his strong commitment to a negotiated solution.

June 1990

I suggested to Mandela that, to celebrate his release, next time we should meet for lunch at the best restaurant in Johannesburg, Linger Longer, then in Braamfontein. It is hard to imagine today the commotion this caused at the time – the intake of breath as we revealed to the proprietor, at the last minute, the identity of our guest and the reactions of the other diners, most of whom had voted to keep him for three decades in jail, as he shook hands with every one of them, as if they were his natural supporters. It was a bravura performance, often to be repeated, and calculated quite deliberately to win over his former opponents. At the end of the meal, characteristically, he dived into the kitchen to thank those who had prepared it.

7 June 1990

De Klerk announced the lifting of the state of emergency in all parts of the country except Natal. He also released a number of ANC prisoners convicted of political crimes and announced an indemnity for the returning exiles.

Pik Botha told me that agreement in principle had been reached with the ANC intelligence chief, Jacob Zuma, on the eventual release of all 'political' prisoners. But he was alarmed at the unexpectedly strong showing by the Conservative Party in a by-election in Umlazi.

The result had been a severe shock to the National Party. If an election were held the next day, he contended, they could not be sure of getting a majority from the white electorate.

15 June 1990

De Klerk wrote to thank the Prime Minister for their meeting at Chequers. He went through all the steps he had taken since becoming President to achieve a 'totally changed South Africa'. He was concerned that the ANC had not yet abandoned the armed struggle and at their continued insistence on nationalisation.

In each of his meetings with me, I had found Mandela practising his classic strategy of seeking to co-opt me, just as he had his warder in jail and the justice minister. The journalist John Carlin, who has written more perceptively than anyone about Mandela, in *Playing the Enemy* and *Knowing Mandela*, describes exactly the same tactics being used on him.[29] I was his advisor, Mandela kept insisting to me and others. I soon found that his next target for co-option was more ambitious. It was in fact the Prime Minister.

Mandela was planning to visit the United States, which would be followed by a visit to London to meet Mrs Thatcher. He called to ask me to meet him at a private clinic in Johannesburg. He had been admitted, suffering from exhaustion. I said that we were extremely worried about his schedule in the US, where he was due to visit seven cities in ten days. To give him some rest before going there, we planned to arrange for him to spend a quiet weekend in the English countryside with his great friend and colleague Oliver Tambo. Mandela was delighted at this gesture.

What he wanted to talk about, however, was how to tackle Margaret Thatcher. I said that I hoped that Mandela would bear in mind that no foreign leader had worked harder for his release and for the unbanning of the ANC. Following De Klerk's speech on 2 February, shots had been fired at the embassy in Pretoria by right-wing extremists, because they considered that the Prime Minister had influenced De Klerk to take these steps. Governments that were unconditional supporters of the ANC had no influence with the South African government. Mandela told me again, as he had said publicly, that, given the influence she could exert, he was determined to get her on his side. He wanted her as an ally and not as an enemy.[30]

I suggested that we should have a rehearsal for the meeting. 'You can be Mandela,' I said, 'and I'll be Mrs Thatcher.' He thought this was an excellent idea. There followed an exchange punctuated by much laughter on both sides. Mandela described the efforts he, Tambo and the ANC had made to engage with the government before he was convicted of treason and that all they were demanding now was a fully democratic constitution. 'You will find us firm allies on all that,' I told him, 'but you must stop all this nonsense about nationalising the banks and the mines!'

I congratulated him on not having used the word 'nationalisation' once in recent weeks. 'But it was your idea,' he said, referring to the influence of the London School of Economics on budding African politicians in the 1950s. 'It was fashionable then,' he added with a smile. It was not fashionable now, I replied, and he should not try this line of argument in Downing Street. I added that, personally, I did not believe that the ANC would end up nationalising anything. We had just been through all this with Swapo. Nationalisation had failed everywhere it had been tried in Africa. Mandela thanked me warmly for these 'tips' for his meeting with the Prime Minister.

During his stay with Tambo, Mandela telephoned Margaret Thatcher. She proceeded, he said, to give him 'a stern but well-meaning lecture'. His schedule was too heavy. He must cut it in half. 'Even a man half your age would have trouble meeting the demands that are being made on you. If you keep this up, you will not come out of America alive!'[31]

Mandela said that the Prime Minister had played a great part in securing his release and that of his colleagues and ensuring that the South African government would sit down and talk to them. Margaret Thatcher said that she hoped that the ANC would now suspend the armed struggle. Mandela replied that the problem was that the South African government seemed unable to restrain the police. But he was totally committed to negotiations, for which he had been struggling for over a decade. If De Klerk removed further obstacles to negotiations, the ANC would announce an end to hostilities. The Prime Minister said that there was no question of lifting the major UN sanctions, but the country needed investment and De Klerk deserved encouragement. The Prime Minister felt 'a bit disappointed' about Mandela's position on the armed struggle.

I responded that, in his meeting with her, Mandela above all was anxious to establish some kind of personal rapport, 'which should not be difficult, given the character of the man'.

CHAPTER XII

---·◆·---

'Free Nelson Mandela!'

4 July 1990

I saw Margaret Thatcher in 10 Downing Street before Mandela arrived. I asked her to remember that he had waited twenty-seven years to tell her his story. This earned me a glare from the clear blue eyes. 'You mean I mustn't interrupt?' she said. Not for the first half-hour, I suggested. Asked if Mandela was anything like Mugabe, I was able to assure her that I had never met two human beings, let alone political leaders, less like each other than Nelson Mandela and Robert Mugabe.

Mandela arrived in the rain with, as we had feared, a mild case of pneumonia. The Prime Minister attempted to revive him with a small glass of port. 'She chided me like a schoolmarm for not taking her advice and cutting down on my schedule', he observed.[32] She then proceeded to listen for almost an hour as Mandela explained to her the history of the ANC and the difficulties he was facing in negotiations. He expressed his gratitude for the pressure she had exerted to help secure his release. She found him, as she wrote in her memoirs, 'supremely courteous, with a genuine nobility of bearing and – most remarkable after all that he had suffered – without any bitterness. I warmed to him.'

She told Mandela that he would get support from the British government in the negotiations for a new constitution. She urged him to suspend the armed struggle – whatever the justification for this, it had now been overtaken – and to meet Buthelezi. Also, she declared, he must stop talking about nationalising the banks and the mines, thereby frightening away all new investment.

As, to her, he still seemed to be stuck in 'some kind of socialist time-warp', over lunch she launched into some home truths about basic economics, with Thabo Mbeki clearly agreeing with her. She concluded that 'South Africa was lucky to have a man of Mr Mandela's stature at such a time. Indeed, I hoped that he would assert himself more at the expense of some of his ANC colleagues.'[33]

Charles Powell's comments on the meeting were that it had taken place in an excellent atmosphere. The Prime Minister already was aware of Mandela's natural dignity. She had been impressed by his courtliness and obvious sincerity. His initial comments had lasted, uninterrupted, for over fifty minutes, 'possibly a record!' He had implied that the armed struggle could be given up quite soon, and believed in De Klerk's integrity. The international community should leave the timing of the lifting of sanctions to the ANC. He recognised that there could not be a constituent assembly before a new constitution was drafted. There were huge economic imbalances which had to be addressed, but the ANC had not decided on nationalisation. They wanted to work with the business community. Margaret Thatcher had concluded the meeting by saying that South Africa was very fortunate to have De Klerk and Mandela at this juncture.

The meeting had gone on for three hours, causing the press assembled outside in Downing Street to start chanting 'Free Nelson Mandela!' Mandela felt that it had gone very well, though he did not, as he observed, make the slightest headway in arguing, very half-heartedly, for more sanctions. He went on to see Labour Party leader Neil Kinnock, who asked how he had got on with the Iron Lady. 'She was warm and motherly,' Mandela replied. 'You must have met some other lady,' Kinnock protested.

At his press conference that afternoon, choosing his words with heavy emphasis, Mandela declared: 'She *is* an enemy of apartheid.' Their differences lay in regard to the methods of inducing the government to dismantle the system. The meeting had been productive and he had come away from it 'full of strength and hope'.[34] His reaction, as he said slyly to me and others, was that the Prime Minister was 'a woman he could do business with!'

July 1990

The South African police uncovered Operation Vula, a secret ANC operation authorised by Tambo in 1986 to prepare the infrastructure for a 'people's war'. The leading operative, Mac Maharaj, was arrested along with other mainly SACP members of the clandestine unit – Pravin Gordhan, Siphiwe Nyanda and Billy Nair. Mandela was taken aback, as he knew nothing of the operation. Joe Slovo told him that it was moribund. In reality, it was regarded by those involved as an insurance policy in case negotiations failed.

I arranged for the Prime Minister to give an interview to Richard Steyn, the liberal editor of *The Star*. It was true, she said, that she had gone out on a limb over South Africa, for instance, in support of De Klerk at the Commonwealth conference in Kuala Lumpur. Now other countries were coming round to her point of view. 'I find I quite often start out on a limb, but eventually find quite a lot of company there.' She spoke warmly about Mandela, but wished that he would stop talking about nationalisation and the armed struggle.

With the ANC still in a state of extreme disorganisation, there followed an episode much appreciated by my colleagues. I had arranged to meet Mandela one afternoon, as scheduled, at his party headquarters in Johannesburg. I arrived there to be told that Nelson Mandela had gone to meet me at the British embassy in Pretoria – where the embassy staff were thrilled to have the opportunity to meet the great man.

As I kept urging the ANC leaders to suspend the armed struggle, I found an unexpected ally in Joe Slovo. Despite the misgivings of his wife, Ruth First (killed in Maputo in 1982 by a bomb despatched by the South African security police), he had defended every twist and turn of Soviet policy since the Second World War. Yet face to face I found him quite a genial, would-be avuncular, character, with a clearer grasp of strategy than many of his colleagues. He understood the need, he said, to demonstrate to De Klerk and his supporters that negotiations could be carried forward in good faith. As Mandela recounts in his memoirs, it was Slovo who proposed, first to him, and then to the ANC politburo, that this step should now be taken, a move he had concerted with Mandela. This was agreed despite some opposition for, as Mandela also observed, MK and the armed struggle had

achieved among ANC supporters a popularity far beyond what had
been achieved on the ground.[35]

This paved the way for a further agreement with the government,
in the form of the Pretoria Minute, signed on 6 August 1990. The
agreement declared that preparatory talks would be held to open the
way to full constitutional negotiations and announced the formal suspension of the armed struggle.

Mandela by now was telling me that he was exhausted. He was
planning to go for three weeks to Cuba, where he could receive some
medical treatment. I said that he had just made a successful visit to
the United States. It would dismay his legion of supporters there if he
were now to spend three weeks with Fidel Castro. Asked if I had any
other ideas, I suggested a stay with his and my friend Enos Mabuza in
Kangwane, alongside the Kruger National Park. This was a great success. He resisted an appeal from Winnie ('Come back, we are at war')
to return to Soweto. I arrived at the embassy one morning to be told
that Mandela was trying to reach me. I telephoned him in Kangwane,
imagining some new crisis in negotiations, only for him to give me the
politically incorrect news that he had succeeded in shooting a blesbok.

September 1990
De Klerk announced that membership of the National Party henceforth would be open to people of all races, a move that represented a
complete break with the history of his party. The polls were showing
that, after Mandela, De Klerk was the most popular figure among
all South Africans. Meanwhile, Jacob Zuma was trying to broker an
agreement with Inkatha to reduce the violence in Natal, though the

ANC continued to insist that Mandela had no plans to meet Buthelezi. An inquiry by the highly respected judge Richard Goldstone censured the police for the March shootings in Sebokeng.

5 September 1990

Meeting with Mandela, I congratulated him on the suspension of the armed struggle. Mandela said again, privately, that he would drop the idea of a constituent assembly. I said that, as the Prime Minister had suggested, we hoped that the government and the ANC would try to reach agreement on constitutional principles before the formal negotiation was engaged. The process still risked being derailed by the violence in the townships. Mandela said that he had been telling ANC supporters that they must not attack the Zulu hostel-dwellers. He accepted De Klerk's sincerity, but the police at lower levels were out of control. There were elements of the security forces who did not want negotiations to succeed and who were supporting or conniving at violence against the ANC.

I said that we welcomed the agreement between Zuma for the ANC and Frank Mdlalose for Inkatha to curb the violence in Natal. Mandela said that he still wanted to meet Buthelezi, but he could not do so in circumstances that would split his party. It would help if Buthelezi could be persuaded to stop making violent statements against the ANC. Would I please speak to Buthelezi? I said that I would speak to Buthelezi, but equally violent statements were being made about him and Inkatha by the ANC.

I said that we would give the ANC some help over the return of exiles and further help with his security. He said that he was committed to the suspension of violence, but that required restraint by the police also. Would I please assure the Prime Minister that he had taken full account of what she had said to him at their meeting? He would not allow the negotiating process to be derailed.

I said that the situation of black South Africans was not really going to improve until the return of new investment. We had noted Mandela's statement that he would not think it necessary to wait for a new constitution to be agreed before proposing the easing of sanctions. We believed that De Klerk was getting close to announcing his intention to abolish all the remaining apartheid legislation. We favoured protection in the new constitution for minority rights, but would not agree with any racially based white veto. Mandela said that he could not advocate the easing of sanctions until the movement was ready for this, but hoped to do so in due course.

I said that I was glad that De Klerk had been given a good reception when he visited Soweto; Mandela strongly agreed. He added that he valued highly Britain's role as what he described as the principal supporter of the negotiating process.

Mandela resumed his punishing schedule of visits abroad, with much effort devoted to fundraising for the ANC. I was conscious of the fact that, among his overseas contacts, I was the one who spent some of my time arguing with him. Most of the others came rather to worship at the shrine. It was a commentary on the quality of this extraordinary man that, far from resenting such expressions of difference, he seemed positively to welcome them and to find them more interesting than unadulterated adulation.

Nearly all our meetings were attended by just him and me.

But on one occasion I went to see him with his and my great friend, Helen Suzman. He had just returned from a visit to Libya. I suggested, politely, that it was not a good idea to have described Muammar Gaddafi as a supporter of human rights. Mandela tried to explain that he had said this because Gaddafi had given money to the ANC, at which point I was brushed aside by Mrs Suzman: 'How could you be so silly, Nelson!' she exclaimed. When, a few months later, Mandela suddenly declared that the voting age should be reduced to fourteen, which he claimed (inaccurately) was the case in Brazil, this earned him another 'Don't be silly, Nelson' call from Helen Suzman.

On another occasion, discussing Inkatha, Mandela suggested that they had the support of only 1 per cent of the population. When I questioned this, he brandished a copy of *The Economist*, which indeed suggested that this was so – on the basis of a survey of the townships in the Transvaal. I replied that if he ever got around to meeting Buthelezi in Ulundi, he would find that in rural, feudal Zululand north of the Tugela, Inkatha commanded 100 per cent support.

As the ANC still contended that Inkatha alone were responsible for the violence, I handed him a photograph of a group of young 'comrades' necklacing a Zulu hostel dweller. Mandela's reaction was: 'But those are not our people.' I pointed to the ANC logos on their T-shirts. Following this exchange, Mandela started to make more and firmer statements calling on both sides to end the violence. It came as a surprise to Mandela that Inkatha won a majority in Natal in the 1994 elections. He acknowledges in *Long Walk to Freedom* that he had seriously underestimated Inkatha's support.[36]

Buthelezi wrote to the Prime Minister to express concern that the ANC were keeping open the possibility of a return to the armed struggle, and that negotiations could not simply be between the government and the ANC. He and Mandela had no trouble with each other personally, but Mandela was under severe pressure from his comrades. On the following day, De Klerk lifted the state of emergency in Natal.

I saw Buthelezi to ask about the discussions with Zuma and the ANC. The latest meeting had been joined by Mbeki. Buthelezi thought that the ANC now realised that they could not just brush Inkatha aside. I raised the issue of violence against Xhosa-speaking workers at a colliery in northern Natal. I said that we strongly supported the inclusion of Inkatha in negotiations. Mandela was rowing backwards on nationalisation. He and Mbeki were firmly committed to a negotiated outcome – with which Buthelezi agreed.

October 1990

William Waldegrave, Minister of State in the Foreign and Commonwealth Office, made what he described as the first 'normal' ministerial visit to South Africa. Leaders from the entire political spectrum had passed through the embassy while he was there. De Klerk would not make the Gorbachev mistake, he felt, of stopping halfway in reform. He did not think that the actual constitutional negotiations would be as difficult as many imagined, as the government were not intending to insist on racially based blocking groups.

8 November 1990

Passing through London, Mandela telephoned the Prime Minister from the ANC headquarters there. He said that he had inquired about meeting her and was disappointed to hear that she was in Geneva. She said that she was delighted to hear from him, and hoped that he was making progress with De Klerk. He said that she could rest assured about this; he would be seeing De Klerk again on 27 November. Both sides realised that a peaceful solution was urgent.

The Prime Minister said that we expected the remaining apartheid legislation to be repealed in the next parliamentary session. Mandela said that the ANC wanted the Internal Security Act also to be repealed. The ANC had two demands – the complete scrapping of apartheid and giving everybody the vote. There was mutual confidence between him and De Klerk.

Margaret Thatcher said that she was pleased that the ANC had suspended the armed struggle and there was less emphasis on nationalisation. Mandela said that he had invited South African business leaders to come up with alternatives to nationalisation. Instability could result from the absence of a fair distribution of resources. She added that she had heard that there would soon be a meeting with Buthelezi, which she welcomed.

Mandela was worried about Renamo-style activity spilling over into South Africa. He was disturbed that De Klerk was not seeking to deal with this problem at its source. She said that Renamo was a terrible organisation, and that we were helping President Chissano to fight it. Mandela said that he knew that Chissano was grateful for our assistance.

The Prime Minister said that Namibia seemed to be doing well; Mandela agreed. She had seen President Nujoma at the UN. Mandela concluded that he was full of optimism and glad to find that the Prime Minister shared it.

12 November 1990

Mandela told me about his telephone conversation with the Prime Minister, who he knew was by then beleaguered within the Conservative Party. I told him that we would help with the resettlement of exiles through the non-governmental organisations we were supporting, as would the EC. Mandela said that he would still like the funding to be given directly to the ANC. I said that would not be possible.

In his statements overseas, Mandela had attributed responsibility for the violence that was taking place exclusively to the security forces. I said that, as a friend, I hoped that he would not continue to do so now that he had returned. I and my staff and the British press all visited the townships regularly. There were many incidents taking place in which 'comrades' claiming to belong to the ANC Youth League were clashing with the supporters of other parties, whether Inkatha, PAC or Azapo, as they had done recently in Bekkersdal and Brandtville.

This seemed to have an effect as, subsequently, he started saying publicly that clashes were taking place between rival black political parties. I added that clashes between ANC supporters and black municipal councillors also posed dangers. We were trying to get the government to announce that they were prepared to move to a non-racial system of local government. Finally, we discussed security at his house, which still needed to be improved.

22 November 1990

When Margaret Thatcher was in the process of being ousted as Prime Minister by her party colleagues, Mandela gave an interview about her to the BBC. In it he said that while they had disagreed about strategy, in particular about sanctions, 'we have much to be thankful to her for'.[37]

'The only alternative to negotiations now is negotiations later'

November 1990

At this point, in another sign of a return to normality, the Foreign Affairs Committee of the House of Commons descended on us in South Africa. I invited them to a dinner in Pretoria at which the entire political spectrum of South Africa was represented, from the Conservative Party, the National Party and Inkatha to the ANC, PAC and the head of Azapo. Next day, Khulu Sibiya in *City Press* inquired why such a gathering could take place only in a foreign embassy, suggesting that South Africans had better start doing more of this for themselves.

We took the committee around the projects we were supporting in the townships, by which they were sufficiently impressed to suggest that the same model of supporting projects directly, bypassing government, should be adopted elsewhere in Africa.

I asked Mandela to meet the committee, which he agreed to do. But he insisted that I should get there in advance and sit on his side of the table, so that I could be introduced as his advisor! The committee paid tribute to the work of the embassy in seeking to build bridges between the ANC and the government and its 'community diplomacy'.

Buthelezi had another meeting with the Prime Minister. She said that Mandela had told Douglas Hurd that he continued to owe a debt of gratitude to Buthelezi for refusing to negotiate with the government while he was still in prison. But he could not go straight for a reconciliation that would split his party from top to bottom. He had to move one step at a time. A meeting between them by now had been delayed for nearly a year.

Also in November, Justice Louis Harms presented his report on the misdeeds of the security forces. This had been commissioned by De Klerk in January, when Magnus Malan had confessed to him that elements of the CCB, which he had created, were out of control. Harms recommended the dissolution of the CCB, which De Klerk approved, only to find out later that the military, contrary to his orders, had kept CCB agents on their payroll. But Harms, to general amazement, dismissed allegations about a death squad operating at Vlakplaas, outside Pretoria, accepting the evidence of its commander, Eugene de Kock, instead.

He did so despite the fact that the activities of this unit were being exposed by Max du Preez and Jacques Pauw of *Vrye Weekblad*. De Klerk was facing a systematic cover-up of these activities by the police and army generals, led by General Kat Liebenberg, head of the SADF who, it subsequently transpired, had himself intervened to protect CCB operatives. Justice Harms had badly failed his country and his President. De Klerk started to rely increasingly on a much tougher judge, Richard Goldstone.

154

December 1990

As John Major took over as Prime Minister, Mandela sent him and the other European heads of government a letter thanking him for his commitment to ending apartheid, but asking that the European Council should defer any easing of sanctions. Chancellor Kohl disagreed; he told John Major that they must do something to help De Klerk, who was 'remarkable, very reliable and taking great risks'.

Oliver Tambo and his wife returned to South Africa on 13 December. I did not go to the airport to meet him as he was bound to be exhausted by the flight. One of my over-eager European colleagues did so instead, only to be told by the anglicised Tambos that they wanted to see 'our ambassador'.

Next day, I went to see them in Soweto. It was a tragedy that Oliver Tambo, by now very frail, had not been able to return to South Africa until so close to the end of his life. Tambo told me that he favoured a meeting between Mandela and Buthelezi. At the ANC preparatory conference, which I attended later in the month, he made a controversial speech in which he called for the ANC's sanctions policy to be reconsidered. The ANC, he said, faced international marginalisation unless it took the initiative to de-emphasise sanctions. Although his speech had been discussed and approved by the national executive, it went down badly with the overheated delegates. Mandela also was criticised for 'personal diplomacy' and for being out of touch with the rank and file.

23 January 1991

Meeting with Mandela. I said that we had been encouraged by his firm stand at the ANC conference in favour of negotiation. We were glad

155

that a meeting with Buthelezi at last had been agreed for 29 January. Mandela said that he was reasonably optimistic about the prospects for negotiations, but De Klerk clearly had problems in carrying the security establishment with him and was not able to control the security forces. He claimed that the police had been given warning about the attacks on ANC supporters in Sebokeng and other townships in which forty-three people had been killed. There were other incidents which led him to question the sincerity of the government, though not of De Klerk himself. Mandela accepted that violence also was resulting from black political rivalries.

Mandela said that in a meeting with De Klerk and Adriaan Vlok, the Minister of Law and Order, Vlok had claimed that the ANC had a double agenda, with the military wing still planning to use force. The ANC had said that they did not trust the government either.

Mandela said that he did not expect miracles from his meeting with Buthelezi, but agreed that it would be psychologically important. I said that the government's attitude mirrored his own about the security forces. They accepted that Mandela and Mbeki were negotiating in good faith, but had legitimate concerns about ANC arms caches and 'self-defence units'.

I said that we had noted Mandela's statement in Lusaka that, if negotiations did not succeed, the ANC would have to 'seize power'. We did not believe that the ANC were in a position to seize power. If negotiations broke down, they would simply have to be started up again. De Klerk appeared to accept this, and I hoped the ANC did too. Mandela said that he did. He was pleased with the remarkable improvement in relations between Britain and the ANC and was grateful for the role the embassy had played in this. He looked forward to meeting John Major later in the year.

In a separate meeting, Thabo Mbeki felt that progress was being made in the discussions with the government. They wanted to move ahead on constitutional principles and some sort of interim council on which the ANC could be represented. Mbeki said that the front-line states would be meeting on 7 February to discuss the maintenance of sanctions. I said that, if they repeated the same old mumbo jumbo about 'nothing having changed', they would lose all credibility. The ANC should be thinking in terms of the selective easing of sanctions. Mbeki said that he realised that EC sanctions were likely to be further eased by June and that the Americans also were likely to move in the course of the year. I suggested a selective relaxation of the sports boycott, now that cricket had a unified governing body; Mbeki was open-minded about this.

De Klerk wrote to John Major to thank him for his role in the decision by the European Council to lift the ban on new investment in South Africa. The security legislation was being reviewed with the objective of ensuring free political participation by all concerned. He was hoping to call a constitutional conference before the end of the year.

1 February 1991

De Klerk announced in his speech at the opening of parliament the repeal of all the remaining apartheid legislation, including the Group Areas Act and the Population Registration Act. John Major wrote to congratulate him on this and to say that we would be looking for a further response from the international community. John Major spoke to the Australian prime minister, Bob Hawke, about the need for progress in lifting sanctions. He found, not to his surprise, that Hawke was mainly interested in getting rid of sports sanctions.

I told Van Heerden that we would be seeking a relaxation of the sports boycott in relation to sports that were integrated and had a unified sports body, such as cricket. The justice department, however, were still making difficulties about some of the exiles, in spite of the indemnity agreed in the Groote Schuur Minute. Mbeki wanted to bring back the two to three thousand people still in Lusaka, and it was in everyone's interests to help him wind up the ANC headquarters there.

Barend du Plessis thanked me for our help in getting a more positive European response, adding that for Kaunda to state that the world must maintain sanctions to 'help De Klerk vis-à-vis the right wing' was fatuous even by his standards. If De Klerk did not get support from the international community, Treurnicht would exploit that against the government.

11 February 1991

Meeting at his office in parliament with De Klerk and Lynda Chalker, Minister of State in the Foreign and Commonwealth Office. De Klerk was pleased that the Europeans had set about lifting sanctions. The ANC were no longer being allowed to dictate their policies. De Klerk said that the ANC had wanted to deal with the government to the exclusion of the other political parties. The ANC's statement on 8 January in favour of a multiparty conference had been a major step forward. It had triggered heavy criticism of Mbeki and other moderates, which Mandela had sought to counter with tough-sounding rhetoric. De Klerk was trying to accelerate the return of exiles through a judicial procedure.

Despite Conservative Party advances, he was confident he could win a referendum of the white electorate. The best help he could get from the outside world would be a rugby tour! We said that lifting the sports boycott would take a bit more time. It might have to be done sport by sport. De Klerk said that, obviously, access to the IMF and external capital was more important. I stressed the need finally to resolve the remaining issues over the release of prisoners. De Klerk expressed strong support for our military actions in the Gulf, where coalition forces were fighting to dislodge Saddam Hussein's forces from Kuwait. He planned to meet the Prime Minister in London in April.

In a meeting with Mandela, he claimed that the EC decision on new investment had made it harder for him to hold his supporters back from mass action. We pointed out that sanctions were crumbling anyway. To maximise their leverage and accelerate the end of apartheid in sport, the ANC should offer to relax sports sanctions in cases where the sports were integrated. Mandela clearly was having to manage tensions within the organisation between Mbeki and the radicals, but said that he was continuing to make progress with De Klerk.

26 February 1991

Dinner with De Klerk. He thought that the exchanges between Mandela and Buthelezi, following their meeting in Durban on 29 January, were doing something towards moderating the violence in Natal. The ANC were backing away from their commitment to nationalisation. In De Klerk's opinion, Mandela knew almost nothing about economics, but

De Klerk spoke warmly of him as a figure of real dignity and authority. He could be rigid and dogmatic, and sometimes his statements did not make sense, but he had to straddle two very different tendencies within the ANC in order to carry his constituency with him.

6 April 1991

Mandela issued a statement accusing the government of complicity in the violence in the black communities and of aiding Inkatha. The government should outlaw the carrying of traditional weapons, dismiss the ministers of Defence and Law and Order, dismantle counter-insurgency units, suspend the police officers in Sebokeng, begin phasing out single-sex migrant workers' hostels and appoint an independent inquiry. If these demands were not met by 9 May the ANC would suspend negotiations and discussion of a new constitution.

April 1991

Steve Tshwete for the ANC and representatives of the sports bodies agreed a constitution for fully unified rugby in South Africa. De Klerk announced that over nine hundred 'political' prisoners had been released. Over four and a half thousand applications for indemnity had been approved for the exiles.

2 May 1991

To try to help break the deadlock, I had lunch with Joe Slovo, regarded as the master strategist by his colleagues in the ANC politburo. Slovo said that the government must phase out the migrant workers' hostels and ban the carrying of traditional weapons. I said that in response to the ANC's 'ultimatum' we had urged the government to offer a multi-party meeting on the violence and a commission of inquiry headed by a judge. The ANC had rejected both proposals and were threatening to suspend talks on the new constitution. 'The only alternative to negotiations now,' I added, 'is negotiations later'. There would be no sympathy for anyone who broke them off. ANC supporters as well as Inkatha were responsible for the violence, and, however poor the performance of the police, the government could not stop them on their own.

Slovo agreed that it was a mistake to have called the ANC document an ultimatum. I said that the idea of arming ANC 'self-defence units' was likely to cause further trouble. They needed to start talking again to Inkatha. Slovo acknowledged that the violence was not benefiting De Klerk. There was some convergence in the government's and the ANC's positions on the constitution and, he agreed, this was the fundamental issue. I said that, the sooner negotiations were started on the future constitution, the easier it would be to manage the transitional problems. I learned afterwards that Slovo had used exactly the same argument with his colleagues on the ANC's national executive committee.

6 May 1991

I telephoned Mandela at his house in Soweto. I told him that we knew that De Klerk had never ordered the killing of anyone, any more than Mandela had done. We were continuing to try to narrow the differences between the government and the ANC on violence. The government were allocating some funds for the conversion of hostel accommodation into family units, but the phasing-out of single men's hostels would take years.

Mandela said that he had been encouraged by a telephone call with De Klerk. But he was adamant that there must be a ban on the carrying of 'cultural' weapons. De Klerk wanted this to be permitted only on genuinely cultural occasions.

I said that the ANC were not going to get satisfaction on all the points in their ultimatum by 9 May (Mandela acknowledged this). It was one thing for them to 'suspend' negotiations on a new constitution which had not yet begun anyway, but they could not afford to break off discussions on the issues of violence, release of prisoners and return of exiles, on which good progress was being made. We had pressed the government to offer an inquiry, headed by a judge. This would put pressure on the police to behave. We wanted the ANC to reconsider their decision not to participate.

Mandela thanked me for the efforts we were making. He would be back in contact with the government, as would Mbeki. The police must learn to deal with black crowds as they would with white ones.

The police, meanwhile, raided a number of hostels, confiscating weapons and putting a strain on De Klerk's relations with Buthelezi. By this time, following the shots that had been fired at the embassy in Pretoria a year before by an extremist faction led by Piet 'Skiet' Rudolph, I was being denounced in the extreme right-wing Afrikaans propaganda sheets as, improbably, the reincarnation of Lord Milner, bent on the destruction of the Boers.

CHAPTER XIV

⟡

'We can hardly drop them on Lusaka or Soweto'

The other cause we had been trying to pursue throughout my time in South Africa was to prevail upon the country to sign the Nuclear Non-Proliferation Treaty and to destroy its small arsenal of nuclear bombs. This was no small ask as, hitherto, no country had ever been prepared to do this. The Americans, too, were working very actively on this cause.

I found a powerful ally in Barend du Plessis. The military nuclear programme by now had cost nearly a billion dollars. Du Plessis could not understand what use South Africa could possibly make of nuclear weapons. 'We can,' as he said to me, 'hardly drop them on Lusaka or Soweto.' Since the inception of the programme in 1974, under Prime Minister John Vorster, South Africa had managed to produce six and a half Hiroshima-type atomic bombs. Their scientists were confident that these would work, though no tests had been conducted.

De Klerk had come to the same conclusion. Nuclear weapons had been intended to deter the total onslaught on South Africa led by the

Soviet Union. With the withdrawal of Cuban forces from Angola, the progressive disintegration of the Soviet Union and the end of the Cold War, he concluded that the massive cost of the nuclear programme no longer made any sense. He moved quickly to close it down. Not long after becoming President, at the end of 1989 he gave instructions for the decommissioning of the enrichment plant near Pretoria at Pelindaba – a Zulu word variously translated as 'end of the discussion' or 'where important matters are settled'.

May/June 1991

On one of the days in this period in which Mandela had suspended negotiations and there was an appearance of deadlock, I spent the evening with him and some of the best jazz musicians from Soweto at the house of his and our friend, Clive Menell. As with Joe Slovo and Thabo Mbeki, I argued that there was no alternative to getting back to negotiations and speeding them up if possible. Mandela said he agreed. He wanted to do more to curb the security forces, but negotiations would be resumed. He wanted there to be discussion of the new constitution by the end of the year.

Mandela, however, was greatly affected by the trial of his wife, which had begun in February. Winnie Mandela was accused following the kidnapping, in December 1988, of four youths and the murder of one of them by members of the Mandela United football club, her bodyguards. The 'football team' had been conducting a reign of terror in Soweto. Mandela kept telling me, and even maintained in *Long Walk to Freedom*, that she was innocent.[38] It was her infidelity, rather than her association with this bunch of thugs, that caused his rift with her. More revealingly, he kept saying that he blamed himself for her difficulties, having been unable to offer her any effective support throughout his years in prison.

My term as ambassador was drawing to an end. Before leaving South Africa, I paid a farewell visit to Bloemfontein to see the wise and humane Chief Justice Michael Corbett. I told him that, while Winnie Mandela might well be found guilty, I doubted if Mandela would be able to cope if his wife were sent to prison. Kobie Coetsee was delivering a similar message to the judiciary, who evidently came to a similar conclusion, as the outcome, on appeal, was a suspended sentence for Winnie Mandela.

As De Klerk had confirmed to me that he would in due course be calling a referendum of the white community to seek support for his policies, I asked to see Mandela with, this time, his spokesman on sport, Steve Tshwete, also attending. I said that we had discussed several times the need to help De Klerk to retain the support of his constituency. De Klerk himself believed that a resumption of international sporting contacts would have more impact than anything else. Could the ANC please start considering selective easing of the sports boycott?

I got a positive hearing. Mandela and Tshwete said that they had started discussing, and would be discussing further, what I was proposing. A few weeks later, they agreed to the readmission of South Africa to international cricket and Olympic sport. It was a decision that paid political dividends. On 17 March 1992, De Klerk won his referendum of the white electorate with 68.7 per cent of the votes, a result universally recognised to have been helped by the fact that a South African cricket team at the time was playing in Australia.

165

Six months before, Margaret Thatcher had been deposed as Prime Minister by fellow members of the Conservative Party. De Klerk regarded it as a debt of honour to invite her to visit South Africa. The visit was bound to be tricky in some respects, as the more militant members of the ANC were threatening to stage demonstrations against her.

In Cape Town, De Klerk gave a state dinner in her honour. During a visit to the Independent Development Trust, the police were alarmed when a crowd gathered outside ... only to burst into applause when she emerged. More predictably, she got a similar reception from the students in the Afrikaner citadel of Stellenbosch.

The ANC secretary-general Cyril Ramaphosa had expressed to me one major worry about her visit. This was that the Johannesburg city council had declared their intention of awarding her the freedom of the city. Ramaphosa warned that, if this happened, there were bound to be demonstrations. I assured him that she had no intention of receiving this award from an all-white council which represented a tiny fraction of the people of Johannesburg. Instead we took her to Soweto, where she got a warm welcome from the nurses at the Baragwanath Hospital and from Aggrey Klaaste at the *Sowetan*.

Having spent two days with De Klerk and his wife at the Mala Mala Game Reserve, I accompanied Mrs Thatcher on the last leg of her visit, to meet Mangosuthu Buthelezi at Ulundi. She was greeted by the usual array of Zulu warriors with their assegais and shields and visited the battlefield on which the British army finally managed to defeat the Zulus on 4 July 1879.

On leaving South Africa she asked me a question which I and others and African governments themselves are still struggling to answer. Given that the independence constitutions in much of the rest of Africa had been honoured more in the breach than in the observance, did I believe that governments in Africa were prepared to accept the Western notion, dating from the eighteenth century, that it was in their own interests to limit their own power and that, however irksome a free press and independent judiciary might prove to be, the alternative was worse? Though she was no friend of the liberation movements, it was thanks to her willingness to take the necessary risks that we had been able to end the Rhodesian war. Throughout my four years in South Africa, I had received no instructions, but full backing from her.

I was now on the verge of leaving South Africa to take up my post as ambassador in Washington, DC. I travelled from Ulundi to Pretoria for a farewell party given by my deputy, Anthony Rowell, who had himself established close relationships with several of the ANC leaders. I arrived to find Mandela there, together with his wife. She was in an ebullient mood, having managed to get herself arrested twice in the course of the day. I was described unkindly by the British press as 'struggling in her embrace'. They were accompanied by Thabo Mbeki, Jacob Zuma and much of the ANC hierarchy.[39] Mandela had made a special effort to make the journey from Soweto, as at the time he still hated visiting Pretoria, where most of his previous experiences had been at police headquarters. Among our other friends there was Johan Heyns.

I told Mandela that we were concerned that the ANC should not paint itself into a corner by making non-negotiable demands at its conference in Durban in July. Mandela asked me to write him a personal note about this, which I did on the following day.

Thabo Mbeki and Jacob Zuma were worried about the temporary ascendancy of the radical wing of the ANC. I said that we had worked hard to persuade the government and Buthelezi to accept the ban on the carrying of assegais by Inkatha supporters in the Transvaal townships. We had tried to help the ANC out of the corner they had got themselves into with their ultimatum, with working groups making progress on issues other than the constitution. The discussion paper I had seen for their conference, demanding a transfer of power to an interim government, was a complete non-starter. Where had this come from?

I was told that it had been put forward by a white SACP faction. Zuma said that Mandela was infuriated about police behaviour and the alleged persecution of his wife, causing him not always to think clearly. It was a tragedy that Tambo was so ill. Would I please make some of these points to Mandela, to help counter the influence of Chris Hani, the youth wing and Winnie?

I paid a farewell call on De Klerk, who said that by 21 June all the apartheid laws would have been repealed. I said that we had helped to persuade most of the neighbouring countries to sign the Nuclear Non-Proliferation Treaty and hoped that South Africa would now do so. De Klerk said that this was imminent. I described the effort we were making to try to ensure that Mandela was not bound into impossible negotiating positions at the ANC conference. However frustrated he might become at times, trying to proceed without the ANC was not going to be a successful course of action. De Klerk agreed with this. He wanted us to go on using our influence with Mandela, Mbeki and Zuma to help ensure that negotiations on a new constitution were engaged by year end.

July 1991

There followed the dismantling and destruction of all the nuclear weapons that had been developed. South Africa signed the Nuclear Non-Proliferation Treaty and opened all its nuclear plants for inspection, thereby becoming the first and only country voluntarily to have dismantled its military nuclear capability. Apart from having opened the way for a fully democratic constitution and removing from the statute book all the apartheid laws, for this decision also FW De Klerk well and truly deserved his Nobel Peace Prize.

The press began publicising the fact that the government had been providing covert support to Inkatha. De Klerk had been aware that two hundred Inkatha members had been trained by the South African military, ostensibly to provide protection to Inkatha leaders at risk of assassination. But, unsurprisingly, it turned out that some of those involved themselves had launched attacks on the ANC, no doubt with the connivance of those who had trained them. Elements of both the police and the army had been responding to appeals from Inkatha for weapons to help them in their fight with the ANC.

De Klerk removed Magnus Malan from his post as defence minister, assigning him to Water Affairs, where it was thought he could not do much more harm. Adriaan Vlok was removed from Law and Order and put in charge of the prison system. In the democratic era, Vlok would apply for amnesty for authorising the attempted poisoning of the ANC-aligned secretary-general of the South African Council of Churches, the Reverend Frank Chikane, whose name was at the head of a death list handed down to him by PW Botha. Vlok was to make a sincere repentance for this scarcely believable crime.

169

De Klerk appointed Judge Richard Goldstone to launch a further, and this time successful, investigation into the dirty tricks departments of the police and army. His discoveries, and those of air force general Pierre Steyn later in the year, led to the 'night of the generals', on which De Klerk dismissed sixteen senior members of the SADF. Clearly, the head of the SADF, General Kat Liebenberg, should have gone as well. But Hernus Kriel, Minister of Law and Order, warned: 'What if they decide to get rid of us instead?' Liebenberg was replaced six months later by General Georg Meiring. When the former head of the army, General Constand Viljoen, told Meiring that they could take over the country in an afternoon, Meiring replied: 'Yes, and what would we do then?' (General Viljoen subsequently was persuaded by Mandela himself to stop thinking in these terms and to participate in the 1994 elections.)

Judge Goldstone was clear in his report that, notwithstanding the contribution made to it by elements of the security forces, the 'primary cause' of the violence was 'the political battle between supporters of the ANC and Inkatha'. Mandela dismissed this as 'superficial'. Although episodically referring to violence from all sides, it was not until 1993 that Mandela fully acknowledged that 'there are members of the ANC who are killing our people. We must face the truth. Our people are just as involved as other organisations in committing violence.'[40]

* * *

Having talked to all the main political leaders over my last few days in South Africa, I left convinced that the process of political change was indeed irreversible and that agreement would be reached on a fully democratic constitution. There would be a lot more violence and turbulence, some serious setbacks and apparent breakdowns. But Mandela and De Klerk knew that in the end they were condemned to agree. I did not believe that De Klerk, having gone this far, would try to stop halfway. I felt sure that in due course we would see an ANC government, led by Mandela, with De Klerk and the National Party participating in it. My main worry was whether an accommodation could also be reached with Inkatha.

When I left, Wits University, on the proposal of Helen Suzman, was kind enough to award me an honorary degree 'for services to the struggle against apartheid'. (The offer from the South African government of the Order of Good Hope I had to decline – on the same grounds Margaret Thatcher had declined the freedom of the city of Johannesburg.) Mandela and Buthelezi added their good wishes, and it was this that pleased me the most, for it demonstrated that, in this deeply divided society, it was possible to try to act as a genuinely honest broker and to retain the confidence of the main participants. This in itself was a demonstration that, in the end, they wanted to try to find a way to agree.

I left with an unaccustomed sense of humility. My predecessors, however hard they tried – and some tried harder than others – could not hope to achieve much in the face of that ironclad regime. And what in the end was achieved was accomplished by and for South Africans – not by any outsider, however well disposed. The most that any embassy could do was to try to help act as a facilitator, and then let South Africans get on with a process in which too much foreign involvement was positively undesirable. For a time the South African government, trying to change but still hard put to bring itself to do so, did feel that it needed one Western country it felt it could appeal to. For a time, Mandela and the ANC also felt they needed someone they could appeal to, with, they hoped, some influence on the other side. Within months, there could be little further need, and certainly much less scope, for such a role.

* * *

Two and a half years later, I was asked by Mandela to fulfil a promise to him that, as soon as he was ready to call for new investment, Britain would be the first to help him to attract back to South Africa some of the companies that had left and to encourage others to invest. This we did at a dinner and reception he addressed at the British embassy in Washington, to which we invited a host of American industrialists and investment fund managers. Throwing away his dreary and partisan prepared speech, as I urged him to do, Mandela declared his intention to seek an accommodation with Buthelezi and to reappoint De Klerk's finance minister, Derek Keys.

Several of the South African businessmen travelling in his wake had been pillars of the apartheid regime. When I congratulated him on his apparent ability to forget this, Mandela replied, with understandable bitterness, that he forgot nothing, and nor did he forgive, but that he needed them now.

A few weeks later, the first fully democratic elections ever to be held in South Africa resulted in a resounding victory for the ANC and in a coalition government in which, despite the tensions between them, all the main political forces for the time being were represented in a still deeply divided society.

The Government of National Unity lasted until May 1996, by which time De Klerk and his colleagues felt that the ANC, with their commanding majority in parliament, had little interest in sharing power and certainly not with their former adversaries. With Mandela installed as President, I was amazed to hear, among others from Anthony Sampson, that he had started saying that he preferred dealing with PW Botha, being supposedly more straightforward, than with FW de Klerk, whom his ANC colleagues continued to regard as a serious political rival. Very exceptionally, I asked to see Mandela, who received me in his office at the Tuynhuys. After the usual greetings, I recalled the meetings I had had, in the same office, with PW Botha, which had entailed arguing, with no success, for his release and for people's lives, for instance those of the Sharpeville Six.

Whatever their disagreements, I reminded him, he should please bear in mind that, but for De Klerk, he would not have been elected President and might still be in jail. Mandela, characteristically, informed his assistant that 'the ambassador is right' (though I had ceased to be one), adding that De Klerk had richly deserved his Nobel Peace Prize, 'for he had made peace possible'.

CHAPTER XV

———— ❖ ————

'We did not join the ANC to become rich; we joined it to go to jail'

During Mandela's state visit to the UK as President of South Africa, in July 1996, he combined with the Prince of Wales to sponsor a musical evening at the Royal Albert Hall. Asked to look after him in the interval, I pointed out that, when it came to the performance by Ladysmith Black Mambazo, the entire audience would be expecting him to get up and dance, as he was accustomed to do in South Africa. Mandela was worried that this might offend the Queen, whom he greatly admired and had taken to calling 'Elizabeth' (not a form of address allowed to anyone else on the planet, except Prince Philip). But get up and dance he did in the Royal Box, with the Duke of Edinburgh following suit – and then the Queen. This was not a feat that could have been accomplished by any other world leader.

When the time came for Mandela to hand over as President, his own preferred candidate to succeed him was Cyril Ramaphosa, secretary-general of the ANC, who had played the leading role in negotiating the new constitution. The party hierarchy insisted on Thabo Mbeki, who had played no less crucial a role in the transition. Mbeki, however, was anxious to step out from the shadow of his predecessor and had anyway been running the government under him. Mandela complained to me and others that, while he could get through to any other world leader, he had difficulty in doing so with his successor, who did not always bother to return his calls.

After he stood down as President, Mandela told me how much he detested Robert Mugabe, whom he regarded as having betrayed everything the liberation movements had fought for. He referred to him derisively as 'Comrade Bob'. Always meticulous about time keeping himself, he also was infuriated by Mugabe's habit of arriving in regal style two hours late for meetings of the Southern African Development Community (SADC). Asked on one occasion what the people of Zimbabwe should do about him, Mandela said: 'If necessary, take up arms!' This earned him some severe remonstrances from the ANC, urging him not to rock the boat, whereupon he fell silent on the subject. In 2000, when the government-sponsored land seizures began in Zimbabwe, however, Mandela told me that, if anything of the kind were to occur in South Africa, he would come out of retirement and 'stop this on the first farm'.

Meanwhile, he did start to criticise the Mbeki government's denialism about HIV/Aids. This led him to discover that his intense loyalty to his party was not always reciprocated. He was summoned to explain himself at a meeting of the national executive committee (NEC) in March 2002. Mbeki did not attend the meeting himself, but Mandela was astonished to find himself being heckled in the meeting by a claque of Mbeki supporters for criticising the government. A furious Mandela never attended another NEC meeting.

The difference between the ANC he believed he represented and its conduct as the ruling party was denounced by his great friend Archbishop Tutu ('they stopped the gravy train just long enough to get on it themselves'). At the 1997 conference in Mafikeng, during which he handed over the presidency of the party to Thabo Mbeki, Mandela railed against corruption. Yet, after standing down as President of the country, to the disappointment of his admirers and despite his own unease, he remained silent about its departures from his ideals. There were many who would have liked to hear him remind his colleagues that, as Kgalema Motlanthe observed of his fellow Robben Islanders: 'We did not join the ANC to become rich; we joined it to go to jail.'

ACKNOWLEDGEMENTS

I am very grateful to Jonathan Ball for suggesting that I should publish this account of numerous meetings with PW Botha, FW de Klerk, Nelson Mandela, Desmond Tutu and others at a crucial time in South Africa's history, and to Jeremy Boraine, Alfred LeMaitre and the team at Jonathan Ball Publishers for their help in producing it. I have been grateful to John Carlin and David Welsh for their suggestions on the manuscript and to Katie Gareh and Marie-France Renwick for their invaluable help with it.

I must especially record my thanks to the Foreign and Commonwealth Office and to the FCO historians Professor Patrick Salmon and Dr Richard Smith for their kindness in enabling me, in writing this book, to review all the reports I sent from South Africa while I was ambassador and the messages exchanged between the Prime Minister, PW Botha and FW de Klerk at the time.

NOTES AND REFERENCES

PROLOGUE

1 Margaret Thatcher, *The Downing Street Years*, HarperCollins, 1993, p. 73.
2 The military wing of Zanu was the Zimbabwe African National Liberation Army (Zanla). The military wing of Zapu was the Zimbabwe People's Revolutionary Army (Zipra).
3 Peter Carrington, *Reflect on Things Past*, HarperCollins, 1988, p. 277.
4 Thatcher Foundation papers, PREM 19/116, 14 August 1980.
5 Thatcher, op. cit., p. 78.

CHAPTER I

6 Theresa Papenfus, *Pik Botha and his Times*, Litera, 2010, p. 341.
7 Thatcher Foundation papers, PREM 19/1392, April 1984.
8 Papenfus, op. cit., p. 348.
9 Geoffrey Howe, *Conflict of Loyalty*, Macmillan, 1994, p. 479.
10 Thatcher Foundation papers, Margaret Thatcher to Archbishop Huddleston, 13 June 1984.
11 FW de Klerk, *The Last Trek: A New Beginning*, Macmillan, 1998, p. 105.
12 Howe, op. cit., p. 490.

CHAPTER V

13 Anatoly Chernyaev, *My Six Years with Gorbachev*, Pennsylvania State University Press, 2000, pp. 99–103.

CHAPTER VII

14 Thatcher, op. cit., p. 529.

CHAPTER VIII

15 David Welsh, *The Rise and Fall of Apartheid*, Jonathan Ball, 2009, p. 384.

CHAPTER IX

16 James A Baker, III, *The Politics of Diplomacy*, GP Putnam's Sons, 1995, p. 223.
17 Nelson Mandela, *Long Walk to Freedom*, Little Brown, 1994, pp. 538–40.

18 George Bush and Brent Scowcroft, *A World Transformed*, Random House, 1998.
19 De Klerk, op. cit., p. 146.
20 John Allen, *Desmond Tutu: Rabble-rouser for Peace*, Rider, 2007, pp. 309–12.
21 Patti Waldmeir, *Anatomy of a Miracle*, Viking, 1997, p. 109.
22 Mandela, op. cit., pp. 542–5.

CHAPTER X
23 Waldmeir, op. cit., p. 157.
24 US embassy Pretoria cable, 30 April 1990, available from wikileaks.org/plusd/cables/90PRETORIA7087_a.html; accessed 14 August 2014.
25 Mandela, op. cit., p. 565.

CHAPTER XI
26 *The Guardian*, 16 April 1990.
27 Welsh, op. cit., p. 389.
28 De Klerk, op. cit., p. 184.
29 John Carlin, *Knowing Mandela*, Atlantic Books, 2013, pp. 21, 80 and 115.
30 See also Anthony Sampson, *Mandela*, HarperCollins, 1999, p. 415. Mandela added these words to the text.
31 Mandela, op. cit., p. 574.

CHAPTER XII
32 Mandela, op. cit., p. 576.
33 Thatcher, op. cit., p. 533.
34 Nelson Mandela, press conference, 4 July 1990.
35 Mandela, op. cit., p. 578.
36 Mandela, op. cit., p. 611.
37 BBC interview with Mandela, 22 November 1990.

CHAPTER XIV
38 Mandela, op. cit., pp. 584–5.
39 *Financial Times*, 1 June 1991.
40 Welsh, op. cit., pp. 413–4.

INDEX

180